THE SOCCER GOALKEEPER

Second Edition

Joseph A. Luxbacher, PhD
University of Pittsburgh

Gene Klein, MEd
PA West Soccer Association
Quaker Valley High School

Human Kinetics Publishers

Library of Congress Cataloging-in-Publication Data

Luxbacher, Joe.
    The soccer goalkeeper / Joseph A. Luxbacher, Gene Klein / --2nd ed.
    p. cm.
    Includes index.
    ISBN 0-87322-397-7
    1. Soccer--Goalkeeping. I. Klein, Gene. II. Title.
    GV943.9.G62L88   1993
    796.334'26--dc20   93-6290
                                        CIP

ISBN: 0-87322-397-7

Acquisitions Editor: Brian Holding
Developmental Editor: Mary E. Fowler
Assistant Editors: Moyra Knight
   and Dawn Roselund
Copyeditor: Wendy Nelson
Proofreader: Kari Nelson
Indexer: Barbara E. Cohen
Production Director: Ernie Noa

Typesetter: Sandra Meier
Text Design: Keith Blomberg
Text Layout: Denise Lowry
Cover Photo: Mitre Sports
Interior Photos: Joseph A. Luxbacher
Interior Art: Keith Blomberg
Printer: United Graphics

Human Kinetics books are available at special discounts for bulk purchase for sales promotions, premiums, fund-raising, or educational use. Special editions or book excerpts can also be created to specification. For details, contact the Special Sales Manager at Human Kinetics.

Printed in the United States of America

10 9 8 7 6 5 4 3 2 1

Human Kinetics Publishers
Box 5076, Champaign, IL 61825-5076
1-800-747-4457

Canada Office:
Human Kinetics Publishers
P.O. Box 2503, Windsor, ON N8Y 4S2
1-800-465-7301 (in Canada only)

Europe Office:
Human Kinetics Publishers (Europe) Ltd.
P.O. Box IW14
Leeds LS16 6TR
England
0532-781708

Australia Office:
Human Kinetics Publishers
P.O. Box 80
Kingswood 5062
South Australia
374-0433

Contents

Acknowledgments

We could not have met the challenge of writing this book without the generous help and support of a number of people. Although it is not possible to list everyone by name, we would like to extend special thanks to the following individuals: Brian Holding, Mary Fowler, and the editors at Human Kinetics for their encouragement and patience; the staff at REUSCH USA for providing the goalkeeper equipment used in the demonstration photos; Sig Brauch, director of referee instruction for the PA WEST Soccer Association, for providing information about the recent FIFA rule changes; and the late Francis Luxbacher for providing his valuable insight regarding the original edition of *The Soccer Goalkeeper*.

The sacrifices made by our friends and loved ones while we traded personal time for writing time will always be remembered and appreciated. Finally, we extend our sincere gratitude to the many fine players and coaches who have contributed to our efforts through their willingness to share thoughts and ideas.

Joe Luxbacher
Gene Klein

Foreword

As a young goalkeeper growing up in New Jersey, I had great difficulty getting the specialized coaching I needed. Although there were many coaches who spent a lot of time with me, seldom did I receive the same attention as the field players.

I quickly learned that goalkeeping is a very specialized position and that the keeper needs tremendous self-discipline and motivation to reach the next level. I attempted to take myself to higher levels by working very hard on my own or with a friend. I learned everything I could through clinics, camps, articles, and books. A book devoted entirely to goalkeeping is needed by coaches and aspiring goalkeepers everywhere. *The Soccer Goalkeeper* is an asset, whatever your experience level, because everyone can learn. It provides invaluable descriptions for the keeper and, at the same time, gives tips and exercises useful for all levels of coaching.

The Soccer Goalkeeper describes all the techniques used by the modern keeper, and I find the descriptions extremely accurate. The chapter on footwork is exceptionally interesting and innovative. The more I compete in professional and international soccer, the more important I find footwork development. The drills given are simple, with no expensive equipment required, and they're unbelievably functional, requiring the use of the foot movements you use in goal.

I consider *The Soccer Goalkeeper* the most thorough and the best-organized book on goalkeeping available. If you're a player who wants to take your game to a higher level, this book will give you the edge. If you're a coach who wants to move your keeper forward, this book will give you the expertise to do it.

Being the goalkeeper of the United States National Team in the 1990 World Cup in Italy was the highlight of my career. I'm eager for the 1994 World Cup, which will be played in my country, the United States. You can reach the dream of becoming the best goalkeeper you possibly can be. It starts right here with this book. I urge you to read it carefully, use the information provided, and enjoy your role as the #1 player on the soccer field.

Tony Meola

About the Authors

Dr. Joseph A. Luxbacher is a former professional player in the North American Soccer League (NASL), the American Soccer League (ASL), and the Major Indoor Soccer League (MISL). He coaches varsity soccer at the University of Pittsburgh and holds an "A" Coaching License from the United States Soccer Federation. Joe also serves as a clinician and speaker at national and regional conventions.

Joe holds a PhD in the management and administration of physical education and athletics and has authored six previous books, including *Fun Games for Soccer Training*, *Soccer: Steps to Success*, and *Teaching Soccer: Steps to Success*. Dr. Luxbacher has also published articles on health and fitness, nutrition and athletic performance, outdoor recreation, sport psychology, and sport sociology. In his leisure he enjoys tennis, canoeing, and photography.

Gene Klein is actively involved with youth soccer on a local and regional basis. He is the head soccer coach at Quaker Valley High School and is also the director of coaching of the PA WEST Soccer Association, an organization of more than 35,000 registered players. Gene was selected as the Region 1 USYSA Boys Coach of the Year in 1990.

Gene holds a master's degree in sport psychology from the University of Pittsburgh. He also holds the Advanced National Coaching Diploma of the National Soccer Coaches Association of America as well as the "A" Coaching License from the United States Soccer Federation. Gene is a former goalkeeper and specializes in goalkeeper training.

Joe Luxbacher and Gene Klein are founders and codirectors of Keystone Soccer Kamps. Keystone Kamps provide specialized instruction and training for field players and goalkeepers. For information on their camp program, contact Joe or Gene at Keystone Soccer Kamps, 509 Upper Road, Pittsburgh, PA 15228.

Preface

To aspiring goalkeepers everywhere

Almost 10 years have passed since we authored the first edition of *The Soccer Goalkeeper*. Since that time soccer has undergone tremendous popular growth in the United States. Millions of boys and girls compete in amateur leagues throughout the country, and that number is growing each year. Soccer also has become one of the most popular participant sports in high schools and colleges. The most obvious sign of soccer's rise to prominence is that, for the first time, the United States has been selected to play host in 1994 to soccer's international championship, the World Cup.

The game of soccer is in a state of perpetual evolution. Systems of play, as well as philosophies of training and coaching, are constantly changing. Just as the game continues to evolve, so does the role of the goalkeeper. Granted, the basics of the trade haven't really changed. The keeper remains the one true specialist on the soccer team, the player whose primary responsibility is to keep the ball out of the net. The goalkeeper must demonstrate a high degree of mental and physical toughness to meet the challenges of a very demanding position. Strength, speed, quickness, and mobility are important assets needed for successful performance. Mastery of basic skills such as diving, boxing, and receiving balls is essential, as is a complete understanding of positioning and tactical concepts.

The modern goalkeeper must go even one step further, however. Today's keeper must be more mobile than ever and undoubtedly will assume even more responsibility and face even greater challenges in the future with the onset of proposed rule changes designed to increase the number of goals scored in a typical soccer game.

The importance of thorough preparation and training cannot be overstated. Through research and practical application, newer and more effective methods of goalkeeper training have been established over the past few years. The second edition of *The Soccer Goalkeeper* addresses the changing role of the goalkeeper and includes essential up-to-date information that will help keepers achieve maximum performance in the match. New and improved illustrations and photos clarify the proper execution of goalkeeper skills. The drills at the ends of chapters develop proficiency in each skill. A new chapter is devoted entirely to footwork. Although footwork in and of itself is not a new aspect of goalkeeping, this book is the first to break footwork down into its eight basic movements. The footwork exercises will enable goalkeepers to improve their coverage of the goal. The chapter dealing with positioning has been expanded to include the role of the keeper/sweeper. A chapter also has been added that discusses how to defend against restart situations, with emphasis on saving penalty kicks. The fitness chapter has been improved to include modern training regimens such as plyometrics.

In short, the second edition of *The Soccer Goalkeeper* is the most comprehensive, well-organized, in-depth discussion of the goalkeeper position available today. Take the material in this book and apply it to your training program. If used as a guide for training, this manual will help raise standards of goalkeeper play to the next level and beyond.

Keep in mind that knowledge and information alone do not guarantee success. Intensive specialized training coupled with playing experience is needed to improve levels of performance. Mastery of goalkeeper skills and an understanding of strategies and tactics will be achieved only through dedicated practice. As coaches and players work together, they will achieve that aim. Coaches can provide the training environment that prepares goalkeepers for the mental and physical challenges of game competition. The goalkeeper must supply the motivation, discipline, and commitment. Through the combined efforts of players and coaches, goalkeepers will reach their maximum potential—an achievement truly deserving of the number 1 player on the soccer field.

CHAPTER 1

Tools of the Trade

The goalkeeper, due to the specific nature of the position, requires special equipment that differs slightly from that of the field players. Basic goalkeeper equipment includes a jersey, shorts or pants, socks, shin guards, shoes, and gloves.

The Goalkeeper Jersey

Goalkeeper jerseys come in a variety of styles and colors. The typical jersey is long-sleeved and made of a durable material. Most are padded at the elbows, and some also over the shoulders and chest. The padding is thin, lightweight, and flexible so as not to restrict movement (see Figure 1.1).

Soccer rules stipulate that the goalkeeper jersey must differ in color from those of the field players. In addition to distinguishing you from teammates, wearing a bright jersey may benefit you in defense of the goal. In some instances an opponent under pressure to quickly release a shot might glance up to locate the goal and instinctively shoot toward the brightest spot (your jersey).

As a rule you should carry two jerseys to the game in case of a color conflict with the opponents. In the event of wet weather or a muddy field,

Figure 1.1   Goalkeeper jerseys are multicolored and usually come with padding in the arms and shoulders.

a jersey change at halftime is also welcome. Due to their construction, goalkeeper jerseys are generally more expensive than the typical field player jersey. Prices range from $35 to more than $100 each.

Shorts and Pants

Most goalkeeper shorts are knee-length "Bermuda-style," which are preferable in game conditions and provide protection against thigh scrapes and abrasions that can occur when you dive to make a save. The fabric is generally nylon or a polyester/cotton blend. Nylon is lighter weight, but polyester/cotton provides greater durability. Most shorts have padding over the hip areas to prevent injury to the hip joint (see Figure 1.2).

Several types of goalkeeper pants are also available. Two common styles are knee-length "knickers" and full-length pants. Both have padding over the hip joints, and the long pants also have padding around the knees. Long pants also have a stirrup at the bottom of each leg through which you slide your foot. Pants are preferable to shorts on hard artificial surfaces, and they are a must for indoor soccer (see Figure 1.3).

Socks

The goalkeeper wears the same style of sock as the field players. The most popular type is the full-footed model that can be pulled up to approximately knee level. Shin guards can be fastened inside the socks.

Figure 1.2 Goalkeeper shorts commonly come in nylon, as shown above, which is lighter in weight. Shorts made of a polyester/cotton blend, however, provide greater durability and wear.

Figure 1.3 Pants, padded at the hips and knees, are essential for training and provide needed protection on hard fields and artificial surfaces.

Shin Guards

Shin guards are generally made of light, flexible plastic and are relatively inexpensive. The guards are positioned underneath the sock and cover the area of the leg between the ankle and knee. Their primary function is to protect against bumps and bruises to the lower leg that may occur during collisions in the goal area.

Shoes

Four general categories of shoes are available, differentiated by their types of sole: molded-sole shoes, turf shoes, screw-in cleated or studded shoes, and flats. The molded-sole shoe usually has a dozen or more medium-length rubber cleats and is most appropriate for soft grass or dirt field surfaces. It is also adaptable for harder synthetic surfaces. The turf shoe has more cleats than the molded-sole shoe, but the cleats are shorter. Turf shoes are most appropriate for artificial surfaces (Astroturf, Omni-turf, etc.) and also hard, dry, natural surfaces. Screw-in, or studded, cleat shoes are generally used to provide optimal traction on soft grass or wet or muddy playing surfaces. Screw-ins have fewer cleats, usually six or seven, than the molded-sole shoes, but the cleats are longer in length. They are not appropriate for hard playing surfaces. Flats are best suited for dry outdoor surfaces or synthetic turf and are most commonly used for indoor soccer.

The quick movements coupled with sudden changes of direction that are an essential part of goalkeeping cannot be accomplished without solid footing. If possible, purchase several types of shoes and use the pair that is best suited for the particular field conditions of the day. Soccer shoes are available in a variety of styles and prices ranging from $30 to $150 per pair. A higher price does not necessarily mean a better shoe. Comfort, durability, and traction are the essential qualities to look for.

Gloves

Gloves have become an essential part of the goalkeeper's equipment. In the past, gloves were used only in the most inclement weather conditions. Most styles were bulky and did not provide a good "feel" for the ball. Improved design and technology have eliminated that liability, however, and today there are gloves available for all playing conditions.

Goalkeeper gloves come in many styles and sizes. Most are composed of leather with a soft foam-rubber palm and have velcro wrist fasteners that secure them tightly to the hands (see Figure 1.4). Most keepers prefer a glove that is slightly larger than the hand, because it increases the grip and also allows the glove longer wear. When selecting gloves, always read the information on the package to determine the type of usage. Prices range from $20 to over $100 per pair.

Figure 1.4   Most goalkeeper gloves are made of leather with a foam-rubber surface on the palm and a slightly padded rubber surface on the outside. The better gloves have velcro wrist fasteners.

Optional Equipment

A variety of optional equipment is also available. Elbow and knee pads, although somewhat bulky, can be used to provide additional protection from the bumps and bruises you could get when you dive to make a save. A second layer of hip pads, sewn into a pair of tights so they fit snugly against your body, can be worn under your goalkeeper shorts or pants.

A baseball-type cap or visor can be worn on days when a bright sun would impair your ability to follow the ball's flight. Become accustomed to wearing a cap in practice before trying it in actual game situations. Helmets have also gained popularity in recent years, particularly among younger players. Most are composed of rubber or plastic and are relatively lightweight (see Figure 1.5). Helmets are especially appropriate for indoor soccer, where the space is more confined and the chances of collisions in the goal area are greater.

Figure 1.5   A foam-rubber helmet sometimes is used for added safety, especially by younger players. Some indoor soccer facilities have made helmets mandatory for goalkeepers.

Developing the Mind and Body

From psychological and physical standpoints, the goalkeeper occupies what may be the most difficult of all team positions. Topflight netminders combine a proper mental approach to the game with outstanding physical ability. One without the other will not suffice.

The Mental Game

For the psychological perspective, we will focus on three important areas of discussion: courage, concentration, and confidence. These components of the "mental game" are commonly referred to as the *Three C's* of goalkeeping.

Courage

Action in the goal area is often fast, furious, and physical. You must be prepared to block point-blank shots, dive at the feet of an onrushing forward to smother a loose ball, or leap up and over opponents to catch a

Figure 2.1   A good goalkeeper makes the most of all her or his physical attributes.

ball dropping into the goal box. To successfully meet such challenges, you must be fearless in defense of the goal.

The goalkeeper must also possess the mental toughness to accept the fact that a single mistake might cost her or his team the game. When a crucial mistake occurs, and invariably it happens to every keeper at one time or another, you must not let it affect your concentration or confidence.

Concentration

Concentration involves the ability to focus total attention on a specific task. A lack of concentration in highly competitive game situations, even for a moment, may prove disastrous. Mistakes by the goalkeeper, more so than errors made by field players, can have a dramatic impact on the psychological state of the team. It is essential that you remain focused at all times and always be ready to make the big save, whether it be in the first or the last minute of play.

Maintaining total concentration throughout a 90-minute match is a difficult task, particularly for younger players who have limited attention spans. Even experienced goalkeepers sometimes lose focus during games in which they handle the ball infrequently. To ensure a high level of concentration, you should begin your mental preparation well before the match begins.

Figure 2.2   The goalkeeper must focus total concentration on the game.

Prematch Preparation

Preparation for the coming match should begin immediately after the last game ends. Performance in game competition generally provides the best measure of your strengths or weaknesses. Analyze your performance, and then strive to improve on the areas of your game that seem to be deficient. Work hard on maintaining concentration during practice sessions. The old coaching adage "You play as you practice" often holds true. Whether it be technical, tactical, or fitness training, always extend yourself to the limit. Intense physical training, in addition to fostering skill development, will have a positive influence on your mental state. If you develop your physical skills to the point where they are almost instinctive, you will be able to focus total concentration on the game and won't have to think much about skill execution.

Another important aspect of prematch mental preparation is analyzing the coming opponent. Ask questions, and then find the answers. Does the opponent team have a particularly dangerous forward? What is its style of play? Does it take shots from well outside the penalty area, or does it try to work the ball in close to the goal? Does it play the flanks and then cross the ball into the goal area, or does it attack directly through the center area of the field? What types of free kick plays and corner kick plays does it use? Answers to these and other such questions will help you mentally prepare for the opposing team's specific tactics and style of play.

Goalkeepers, just like everyone else, are individuals with different personalities and motivations. As a consequence there is no surefire program you can use before the game to ensure optimal mental preparation. What works for one keeper might be totally inappropriate for another. For example, some goalkeepers prefer to arrive at the park hours before the game; others prefer to arrive at the last possible moment. Some prefer total relaxation and quiet prior to the match; others prefer to be active and vocal.

Regardless of individual preferences, however, there are several specific tasks that all goalkeepers should perform before the game to familiarize themselves with field conditions. Visually inspect the goal areas and field surface. This will enable you to select the proper equipment (e.g., shoes, gloves) for the playing conditions. Note the position of the sun and the path it will follow as the game progresses. This will help you decide whether to wear a hat or sun visor. Take into account wind direction and velocity when deciding on which method of distribution to use. Get a feeling for the attitude of the spectators. Are they friendly or hostile? The more acclimated and comfortable you become with the game environment, the easier it will be to concentrate on the game.

Concentration During the Match

Soccer is a game of improvisation—spontaneous and for the most part unrehearsed—so you must become totally immersed in the game from the opening whistle. Experience every pass, feel every tackle. Block out potential distractions such as poor field conditions, inclement weather, partisan crowds, or opponents who verbally question your fortitude.

Although you should be aware of virtually everything that occurs during the game, focus your attention on three primary aspects of play:

- *Position of the ball:* Constantly be aware of the ball and its relative position to the goal. Your concentration level must be high when opponents have possession of the ball within your team's half of the field. A high degree of readiness is required when opponents have possession of the ball and are within striking distance of the goal.
- *Movement of opponents:* Always keep a close eye on movement of opponents, particularly of those positioned in and around the penalty area. This will enable you to anticipate and position accordingly.
- *Organization of the defense:* Verbal communication with teammates can effectively improve teamwork and create a strong defensive unit. From your vantage point behind the defense, you are in an excellent position to assist defenders in their positioning with relation to the ball and opponents.

Confidence

Confidence in one's ability is essential for successful athletic performance. A high degree of self-confidence is of particular importance for the goalkeeper. Confidence can be developed through intense mental and physical preparation. Teammates should also have confidence that the goalkeeper can do the job. There are several ways you can instill greater confidence in your teammates.

- *Dominate the box:* The penalty box is your domain, and you should make everyone in the park aware of it. Do not be timid or hesitant in your actions.
- *Verbally take charge:* Do not hesitate to issue commands to teammates. This does not imply that continuous chatter is a desirable characteristic of topflight netminders—it definitely is not! Informative communication is necessary, however. Communicating with teammates will also help you to stay mentally focused on the game.
- *Demand the ball:* Demonstrate through actions as well as words that you want to handle the ball. Be active within the penalty area, and attempt to field any shot or cross within your reach. Indecisiveness on your part can breed confusion and a lack of confidence from your teammates.
- *Psych opponents:* You may be able to gain an edge over opponents even before the game begins. For example, some keepers conduct their pregame warm-up in full view of the opposing team, using quick-reaction saves and acrobatic dives to make opponents doubt their ability to score.

The Physical Game

Mastery of the mental game is only half the battle. The goalkeeper must also possess the physical talents required to successfully play the position. Although goalkeepers do not necessarily come in any specific size or shape, several important physical attributes seem to be characteristic of topflight netminders.

Hands

The ability to catch and hold the ball is of critical importance. Mishandled shots usually result in goals against your team. Although the size of a goalkeeper's hands is not of particular significance, larger hands certainly provide an added advantage. Of greater importance is the development of "soft hands," which cushion and hold even the most difficult shots. You can improve your ability to catch the ball through repetitive practice in receiving shots and through a variety of ball-handling exercises (see pages 59-72). Wrist and hand strength is also important and can be developed and improved through strength-training exercises.

Height

All other things being equal, a tall goalkeeper would seemingly have a decided edge over a shorter individual. However, rarely are all other things equal, and a lack of height does not necessarily prevent a player from becoming a top goalkeeper. A short individual may compensate for lack of height by improving leaping ability and by developing excellent technique.

Strength

Overall body strength is important. The keeper must be able to vault through the air with the skill of an acrobat. You need strong arms, shoulders, and chest to stop shots when you are fully extended. Sufficient upper body strength also enables you to distribute the ball over long distances by throwing. You need powerful legs when you dive and when you leap up to challenge opponents for high balls. Leg strength is also a factor when punting the ball. A variety of strength-training exercises are listed in chapter 11.

Flexibility

The goalkeeper may be required to extend her or his body in a variety of ways when receiving balls. Overall flexibility is a must and can be developed or improved through static stretch exercises (see chapter 11).

Mobility/Footwork

Balance, quickness, speed, and proper footwork are essential for the goalkeeper to cover the largest possible area of the goal. Goalkeeper footwork is discussed in detail in chapter 3.

CHAPTER 3

Extending Range Through Fundamental Footwork

Footwork can be defined as the foot movements used to extend all aspects of the goalkeeper's range. Proper footwork enables you to expand your control of the goal and penalty areas. Through improved mobility you not only will be able to stop more shots, but you also will be able to prevent certain shots from being taken. Developing proper footwork, therefore, should be a primary focus of your training.

The basic goalkeeper stance, or starting position, for all foot movements is called the "ready position." From the ready position you can best execute the eight essential foot movements. Each technique is used for a specific purpose and game situation. The foot movements you should master are the side shuffle, collapse step, power step, drop step, drop step/crossover step, crossover sprint, backpedal, and vertical jump.

Figure 3.1 By keeping your weight balanced and centered over the balls of your feet, you are prepared to move quickly in any direction to make a save.

The Ready Position

Assume the ready position (see Figure 3.1) whenever an opponent with the ball is within striking distance of the goal. Place your feet approximately shoulder-width apart with toes pointing toward the ball. Center your weight over the balls of your feet with heels slightly elevated. Hold your head and upper body erect, with your knees slightly flexed. Position your hips and buttocks as if you were sitting on a medium-height stool. Hands are carried at approximately waist level, with palms forward and fingers pointed upward. Keep your head steady, and focus your vision on the ball. From the ready position you will be able to move quickly in any direction.

KEY ASPECTS OF PERFORMANCE

The Ready Position

- Assume this position before the shot is taken.
- Maintain balance and body control.
- Center your weight over the balls of your feet.
- Maintain an erect posture; do not lean too far forward.
- Assume a comfortable and relaxed stance.

The Side Shuffle

Figures 3.2, 3.3   The side shuffle is used to align the body with the ball (Figure 3.2). Correct execution involves pushing off with the toes and bringing the feet together, but not crossing them (Figure 3.3).

Use the side shuffle when you move sideways to align your body with the ball. Never cross your feet when shuffling. Maintain good balance, with your weight centered over the balls of your feet (see Figures 3.2 and 3.3).

The advantage of shuffling sideways, rather than running, is that you can remain in the ready position and also maintain balance and body control. This enables you to quickly set for a shot, suddenly change direction in response to the changing position of the ball, or quickly readjust your body position to make a reaction save. The more quickly you can shuffle sideways, the greater the area of the goal you will be able to cover.

Practicing Your Footwork

Practice shuffling from one goalpost to the other along an imaginary arc. When you feel comfortable with the foot movement, begin to field shots as you shuffle sideways.

The Collapse Step

Figures 3.4, 3.5 The collapse step is used when saving ground balls. Step toward the ball and rotate your ankle inward (Figure 3.4). Collapse your leg at the knee, and fall to the ground on your side (Figure 3.5).

Use the collapse step when fielding rolling balls immediately to your side. To save, you must get to the ground very quickly. The initial movement is made with the foot nearest to the ball. Step toward the ball, rotate your ankle inward, and collapse your leg at the knee. Fall to the ground on your side. As you land, the lower leg (side of calf) contacts the ground first, followed by the thigh, hip, and upper body, in that sequence (see Figures 3.4 and 3.5).

Practicing Your Footwork

Position yourself between two balls placed approximately 8 yards apart. Shuffle sideways to a ball, execute a collapse step, fall, and pin the ball to the ground with both hands. Get up, shuffle sideways to the other ball, and repeat the collapse step.

The Power Step

Figures 3.6, 3.7   The power step is used to vault across the goal. Take a short step to the ball with the foot nearest the ball (Figure 3.6). Simultaneously, thrust your opposite arm and leg in the direction of the dive (Figure 3.7).

Proper execution of the power step will enhance your ability to vault across the goal. Take a short, sideways step with the foot nearest the ball, flex your knee, and push off in the direction of the dive. Simultaneously thrust your opposite leg upward (see Figures 3.6 and 3.7). The opposite arm follows suit to generate momentum in the direction of the dive.

Practicing Your Footwork

Figures 3.8, 3.9   Practice the power step by stepping to a ball or another obstacle (Figure 3.8) and vaulting over it (Figure 3.9).

Stand about 1 yard from a stationary ball. Take a power step toward the ball, flex your knee, and vault sideways over the ball (see Figures 3.8 and 3.9). Repeat the technique in the opposite direction.

The Drop Step

Figures 3.10, 3.11   Use the drop step to save a ball falling behind you. From a ready position (Figure 3.10), open your hips by taking a step backward with the foot nearest the ball (Figure 3.11).

Use the drop-step technique to turn a ball that is dropping behind you over the bar. From the ready position, immediately open your hips by taking a step backward with the foot nearest the ball. For example, if the ball is dropping over your right shoulder, you should drop-step with your right foot (see Figures 3.10 and 3.11). The drop step enables you to quickly get closer to the goal line while still keeping the ball in sight at all times. It also rotates your hips and upper body in preparation to turn the ball over the bar.

Practicing Your Footwork

Do the "drop-step shuffle." Stand on the front edge of the penalty area with your back to the goal. Take a drop step to the right, then shuffle once. Rotate your upper body and hips in the opposite direction, and drop-step to the left. Shuffle once, and then drop-step right. Continue the drop-step sequence (right, left, right, etc.) until you reach the end line of the field. Repeat the exercise again, this time beginning on the end line and moving out toward the edge of the penalty area. Keep your head steady and buttocks low to the ground while you execute the drop-step shuffle.

The Drop Step/Crossover Step

Figures 3.12, 3.13   To perform the drop step/crossover step, take a drop step with the foot nearest the ball (Figure 3.12), and immediately follow it with a crossover step with the opposite foot (Figure 3.13). Keep your head and eyes focused on the ball.

The drop step/crossover step is used when you have been caught too far out of the goal and must immediately get back to the line. Execute a drop step followed immediately by a crossover step with the opposite foot. This movement will enable you to quickly achieve depth (drop step) and distance (crossover). The drop step must initiate the movement and be followed by the crossover; reversing the order of steps won't work! Focus your vision on the ball while you retreat toward the goal line. It is also important that you angle your shoulders and hips toward the field (see Figures 3.12 and 3.13).

Practicing Your Footwork

Do the "drop-step/crossover-step shuffle." Stand on the front edge of the penalty area with your back to the goal. Take a drop step and then a crossover step with the opposite foot. Square your hips, then execute a drop step/crossover in the opposite direction. Square your hips, repeat, and continue until you reach the end line. Turn around and repeat the sequence of foot movements as you return to the edge of the penalty area.

The Crossover Sprint

Figures 3.14, 3.15   Use the crossover sprint when you are caught well off line and must recover quickly. After initiating the drop step/crossover step, continue the crossover movement while sprinting to the goal (Figure 3.14). This method allows your head, shoulders, and hips to remain angled toward the ball (Figure 3.15).

Use the crossover sprint when you have been caught well off of the goal line and the ball has been lobbed over your head. Initiate the movement with a drop step/crossover step immediately followed by a sprint toward the goal line. Don't turn your back to the ball while you sprint. Angle your head, shoulders, and hips toward the field, with your vision focused on the ball (see Figures 3.14 and 3.15).

Practicing Your Footwork

Start at the left front edge of the penalty area. Take a drop step/crossover step, and execute a crossover sprint to the right goalpost. Jog back to the opposite front edge of the penalty area, and repeat the crossover sprint to the left goalpost.

The Backpedal

Figures 3.16, 3.17   The backpedal generally is employed in finishing a crossover sprint. If you can recover and catch the ball (Figure 3.16), position your hips square to the ball as you receive it (Figure 3.17).

Use the backpedal when you are preparing to catch a lofted ball rather than turn it over the bar. This foot movement is often observed at the end of a crossover sprint. It is used rarely as a recovery technique but rather as the finishing leg of a recovery run.

You won't need to use the backpedal technique very often if you use the drop step, the drop step/crossover step, and the crossover sprint effectively. This technique differs from these other foot movements in that your hips, shoulders, and head remain square rather than angled to the ball. Use short, choppy steps as you backpedal, with your weight centered over the balls of your feet. Your buttocks should remain low to the ground, with your upper body leaning slightly forward for optimal balance (see Figures 3.16 and 3.17).

Practicing Your Footwork

Begin on a touchline (sideline) of the field. Jog toward the opposite touchline for a few yards. On command, quickly turn 180 degrees and backpedal several yards, then turn and jog, turn and backpedal, and so on. Continue the exercise, moving across the field from touchline to touchline. Increase your speed for each repetition.

The Vertical Jump

One of the objectives of proper footwork is to increase all aspects of the goalkeeper's range. This includes your range up into the air as well as side to side. At times you will have to jump up and over opponents to catch a high ball dropping into the goal area. Use the one-leg takeoff technique when jumping to catch a crossed ball (see chapter 5, page 57). A two-leg takeoff can be used when you jump up to catch a high ball coming directly at you. You can increase the height of your vertical jump through proper footwork and through the use of the plyometric and strength-training exercises discussed in chapter 11.

Practicing Your Footwork

Figure 3.18   By jumping onto and off of a bleacher or fixed bench (using one- and two-leg takeoffs), you can increase the height of your vertical jump.

From a standing position, jump up onto a bleacher or fixed bench, then jump back to the ground (see Figure 3.18). Repeat for 30 seconds, then rest. Use both one- and two-leg takeoffs (see chapter 11, page 145).

Drills

The following drills are designed to improve your footwork. Most combine several different footwork movements, making optimal use of your training time. All exercises should be clearly explained and demonstrated to you before you practice them. It is important that you do sufficient repetitions until you have mastered the movement. Most exercises are organized to simulate conditions that occur in and around the goal area and may be adapted to suit your own needs and abilities.

Coaching Point for All Drills

Progress slowly through the following drills in order to observe any technical flaws. Once the goalkeeper has demonstrated confidence in executing the various foot movements under relatively little pressure, increase the physical demands by increasing either the number of repetitions, the speed of repetition, or both.

Jump and Turn

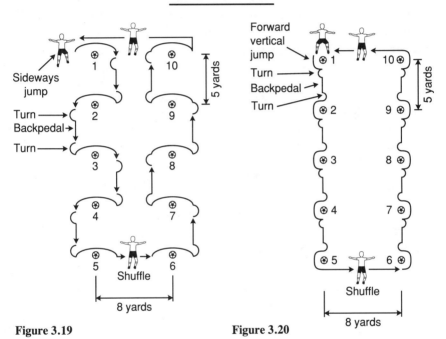

Figure 3.19   Figure 3.20

Equipment: 10 balls

Organization: Position 5 balls in a straight line, with 5 yards' distance between balls. Position an identical line of balls parallel with the first line, about 8 yards away. Number the balls 1 through 10. This drill emphasizes the vertical jump, drop step, backpedal, and shuffle movements.

Procedure: The goalkeeper stands next to Ball #1. He or she uses a vertical jump to leap sideways over the ball, immediately turns using a drop step, backpedals to the next ball, turns again, and vertically jumps sideways over Ball #2 (see Figure 3.19). The goalkeeper should not cross the legs or turn in a circle when preparing to jump. The goalkeeper continues through the circuit to Ball #5, then shuffles sideways in the ready position until reaching the second line of balls. The keeper performs the sideways vertical jump over Balls #6 through #10, shuffles back to the first line of balls, and repeats the circuit. Continue for three repetitions of the circuit.

Variation: This drill emphasizes the vertical jump, drop step, backpedal, and shuffle movements. Use the same basic setup and procedure as in the previous drill, except that the goalkeeper uses a forward jump rather than a sideways jump to clear the balls (see Figure 3.20). After jumping over Ball #1, the keeper should rotate the hips, take a drop step, backpedal to Ball #2, turn, execute a forward jump, and then continue on to Ball #3, then repeat the movement sequence through Ball #5, shuffle across to Ball #6, and repeat the sequence through Ball #10. The goalkeeper should not cross her or his legs or turn in a complete circle at any time.

Power Step and Fly

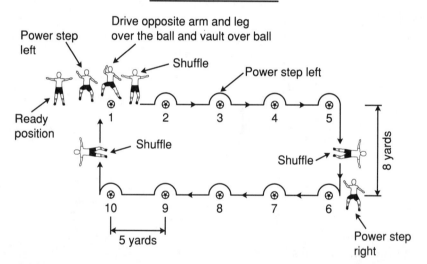

Equipment: 10 balls

Organization: Position balls as in the preceding Jump and Turn drill. This exercise emphasizes the power step and shuffle movements.

Procedure: The goalkeeper takes a power step left, jumps over Ball #1, shuffles sideways to Ball #2, takes a power step left, jumps over Ball #2, and continues through the circuit to Ball #5. The goalkeeper then shuffles across to the opposite line of balls and repeats the movement sequence of power step, jump, and shuffle. Use a power step right when jumping over the second line of balls. Repeat the circuit four times.

Variation #1:   The same organizational format as in the Jump and Turn drill, except that the keeper alternates using a right and then left power step when moving through the circuit of balls. This is accomplished by rotating the hips during the shuffle.

Variation #2:   The same as Variation #1 except that the number of balls and the distance between them should vary, ranging from a minimum of 3 yards to a maximum of 15 yards.

Drop Step and Fly

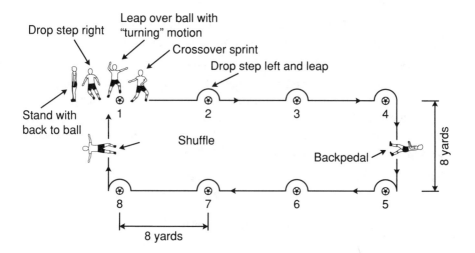

Equipment: 8 balls

Organization: Place 4 balls in a straight line with 8 yards' distance between balls. The other 4 balls are in a straight line parallel with the first line. This drill emphasizes the drop step, crossover sprint, and backpedal movements.

Procedure: The goalkeeper stands with her or his back to the first ball. The keeper takes a drop step right, plants the foot, and leaps over the ball as if turning a ball that is dropping over the right shoulder over the bar. Upon landing the keeper rotates hips to the left and uses a crossover sprint to the next ball, takes a drop step left, plants foot, and leaps over the ball as if turning a ball that is dropping over the left shoulder. Continue through Balls #3 and #4, then backpedal to the opposite line of balls, and repeat the sequence with Balls #5 through #8. Repeat the circuit four times.

Fast Footwork

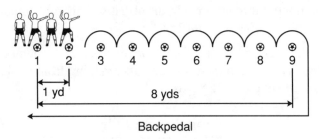

Equipment: 9 balls

Organization: Place 9 balls in a straight line with 1 yard's distance between balls. This exercise places emphasis on quick feet.

Procedure: The goalkeeper stands sideways in the ready position beside the first ball. On command the keeper steps over the first ball, then the second, and so on through the entire circuit of balls. When stepping over a ball the lead foot should leave the ground first, followed immediately by the trailing foot. After reaching Ball #9 the keeper should backpedal to Ball #1 as quickly as possible. Repeat the circuit several times.

Variation: The keeper executes the drop-step shuffle instead of the backpedal when returning to Ball #1 after completing the circuit.

Power Step and Shuffle

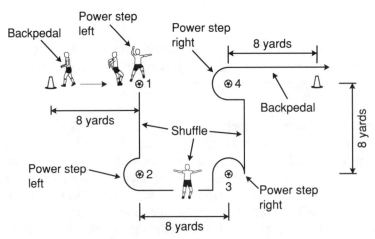

Equipment: 4 balls, 2 cones or markers

Organization: Place 4 balls in a square with 8 yards' distance between balls. Place 2 cones in a straight line about 8 yards from two of the balls. This drill requires the power step, shuffle, and backpedal movements.

Procedure: The goalkeeper begins at a cone and backpedals to Ball #1, turns, and executes a power step left over Ball #1. The keeper immediately shuffles left and executes a power step left over Ball #2. The keeper then rotates hips, shuffles right, and executes a power step right over Ball #3. The goalkeeper continues to shuffle right and executes a power step right over Ball #4. The keeper then quickly backpedals to the opposite cone and repeats the circuit in reverse order.

Variation: The goalkeeper performs same procedure but replaces the backpedal with the crossover sprint movement.

Combination Footwork

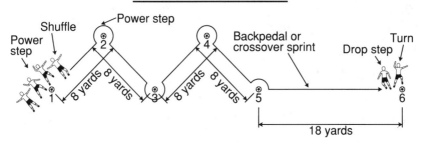

Equipment: 6 balls

Organization: Place Balls #1 through #5 in an *M* layout with 8 yards distance between balls. Place Ball #6 about 18 yards from Ball #5. This drill requires the goalkeeper to execute all foot movements learned thus far.

Procedure: The goalkeeper positions beside Ball #1. He or she begins by taking a power step over Ball #1, shuffles to Ball #2, takes a power step, shuffles to Ball #3, repeats, and so on, until passing Ball #5. At that point, the keeper quickly turns and backpedals to Ball #6. When nearing Ball #6, the keeper takes a drop step, then leaps over the ball as if turning a ball over the bar.

Variation #1:   After each power step the keeper rotates her or his hips when shuffling to the next ball. In this manner the keeper can alternate power steps with the left and right feet.

Variation #2:   Instead of backpedaling to Ball #6, the goalkeeper takes a drop step/crossover step and uses the crossover sprint.

Fast Backtracking

Figure 3.21   Figure 3.22

Equipment: 10 to 15 balls, 1 regulation-size goal

Organization: A goalkeeper and a server (with balls) position in front of a regulation-size goal. The keeper stands with back to the goal while the server faces the goal. This drill requires the drop step, drop step/crossover, crossover sprint, and backpedal movements.

Procedure: The goalkeeper positions 3 yards in front of the goal (see Figure 3.21). On command he or she takes a drop step with the left foot, rotates hips and shoulders, extends right arm and touches right hand to the crossbar as if turning a ball over the bar (see Figure 3.22). Repeat the exercise using the drop step with the opposite foot. The server is not included in this portion of the drill.

Variation #1:   The keeper stands 6 to 8 yards in front of the goal. On command she or he executes a drop step with the left foot, follows with a quick crossover step with the right foot, squares the hips, and backpedals to the goal. Repeat the exercise using the opposite foot to drop-step. The server is not included in this portion of drill.

Variation #2:   The keeper stands 8 to 12 yards in front of the goal. On command he or she uses a drop step/crossover step followed by a crossover sprint to the goal. When nearing the goal line, the keeper executes a drop step with the right foot, rotates hips and shoulders, extends the left arm and touches the left hand to the crossbar as if turning a ball over the bar. Repeat the exercise using the opposite foot to drop-step. The server is not included in this portion of the drill.

Variation #3:   The keeper stands 8 to 12 yards in front of the goal. On command she or he executes a drop step/crossover step, followed by a crossover sprint to the goal. Approximately 3 yards from the goal line, the keeper squares hips and backpedals to the line. Repeat the drill using the opposite foot to drop-step. The server is not included in this portion of the drill.

Variation #4:   Once the goalkeeper has developed confidence in his or her footwork, add a server to Variations #1, #2, and #3. For all exercises the server should toss a lofted ball over the goalkeeper's head toward the crossbar.

Power Jumping

Equipment: 9 balls

Organization: Place 9 balls in a straight line with 1 yard's distance between balls. The goalkeeper stands facing the first ball. This exercise emphasizes the vertical jump movement.

Procedure: On command the keeper jumps forward over Ball #1, then jumps backward over Ball #1, then jumps forward over Ball #1 again. The keeper repeats the same jumping sequence over Ball #2, then Ball #3, and so on, until reaching the last ball.

Variation: Keeper jumps forward over two balls, then jumps back one, then forward two, back one, and so on, continuing through the line of balls.

CHAPTER 4

Positioning for Maximum Coverage

Positioning is the physical posture of the goalkeeper as well as her or his position in relation to the ball. It is important that the goalkeeper understand the various aspects of positioning in order to provide maximum coverage of the goal area. As discussed in chapter 3, the basic goalkeeper stance (the ready position) ensures optimal balance and distribution of weight. Assume the ready position whenever an opponent with the ball is within striking distance of the goal. From this posture you will be able to move quickly in any direction.

Positioning in relation to the ball is referred to as "angle play." The basic tenet of angle play is that the goalkeeper, by moving forward from the goal line toward the ball and then sideways along an imaginary arc that connects both goalposts, can reduce the shooting angle and thus expose less of the goal. The discussion of angle play in this chapter focuses on positioning for shots taken from outside of the goal area. Positioning for breakaways is discussed in chapter 8.

A relatively new aspect of goalkeeper positioning involves the role of the keeper/sweeper. At times the goalkeeper must leave the penalty area to intercept the opponent's passes directed into the vital space behind the last line of defenders. When doing so, the keeper must play the ball with his or her feet.

A final aspect of positioning is the art of communicating with teammates. The keeper is in an excellent position to view the entire field and from that vantage point can provide important information that can help in the organization of the team defense.

The Keeper's Arc

You must be on constant alert when an opponent is within shooting range. Most goals are scored from the area front and center of the goal (see Figure 4.1). Whenever the ball is within this dangerous scoring area you should position yourself about 2 to 6 yards in front of the goal line, depending upon the distance of the ball from the goal. Never stand on the goal line except in the case of a penalty kick. In that instance game rules specify that you must be on the goal line until the ball is kicked.

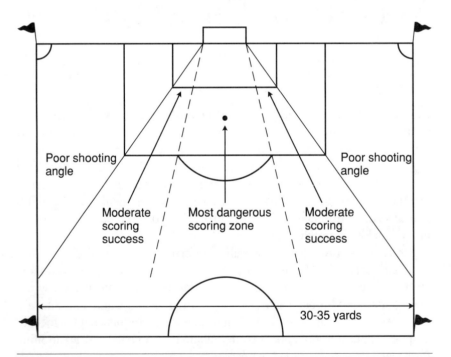

Figure 4.1   Most goals are scored from the shot taken in the area in front and center of the goal, where a wide shooting angle is provided.

As the ball changes location, adjust your position accordingly by moving along an imaginary arc connecting the two goalposts. This line is commonly referred to as the "goalkeeper's arc" (see Figure 4.2). Proper footwork is essential for you to move smoothly and quickly along the arc. Use the side shuffle movement discussed in chapter 3. Avoid crossover movements, which tend to limit your ability to quickly change direction in reaction to a shot. As the ball moves toward the flank area, shuffle along the arc and position closer to the near post. Extend your arm to feel for the post as you approach it. Your vision should remain focused on the ball at all times. As the ball moves closer to the end line of the field, the likelihood of a shot decreases due to the poor shooting angle. In that situation, leave the near post and move to a more central position in anticipation of the cross.

How far should the imaginary arc extend in front of the goal line? There is no definite answer to that question; it depends upon your ability and the position of the ball. Developing good footwork and mobility will

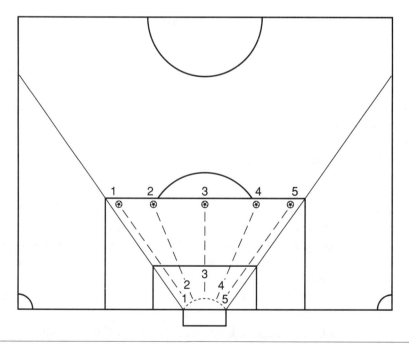

Figure 4.2   As the position of the ball shifts, you must adjust accordingly. The numbers (1 to 5) along the goalkeeper's arc demonstrate your correct positioning in relationship to the changing position of the ball.

enable you to extend the arc a greater distance from the goal line without becoming vulnerable to a ball lobbed over your head.

KEY ASPECTS OF PERFORMANCE

The Keeper's Arc

- Shuffle sideways in a semicircular path extending from post to post.
- Never cross your feet when shuffling.
- Focus your vision on the ball at all times.
- Extend your arm and feel for the near post.
- Readjust your position along the arc to correspond with the changing position of the ball.
- Remain in a ready position as you shuffle along the arc.

Angle Play

One of the most difficult decisions you will face is deciding how far to advance off the arc as you prepare to make a save. Although moving too far forward may leave you vulnerable to a chip (lob) shot, you must not be afraid to leave the security of the goal line to reduce the opponent's shooting angle (see Figures 4.3 and 4.4). It is important not to rush forward too fast or too soon as you advance toward the ball. Use a forward shuffle movement and avoid long strides, which will tend to limit your mobility.

Assume a semicrouch position as you get closer to the ball. From this posture you will be able to quickly react to the low hard shot, one of the most difficult to save. From the semicrouch you are also able to get to the ground quickly to smother the ball, should the opponent dribble in on the goal rather than shoot. The proper technique for smothering a breakaway is discussed in chapter 8.

Angle play is difficult to execute successfully, because every situation is unique. Although actual game experience is the optimal environment for learning angle play, practice situations can also be structured that simulate the pressures encountered in game competition. It is only through repetitive training in simulated game conditions that this essential element of goalkeeper play can be mastered.

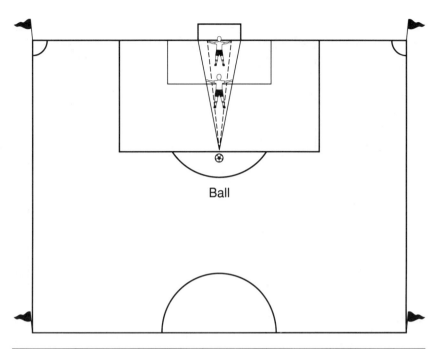

Figure 4.3   An imaginary triangle can be formed with sides extending from the ball to each goalpost. As you move off the line, advancing toward the ball, the angle is narrowed. Ideally, you should be in a position to bisect the angle, from which point you can cover the entire goal.

KEY ASPECTS OF PERFORMANCE

Angle Play

- Know the area; be aware of your position in relation to the ball and the goal.
- Use the side shuffle to move laterally; use the forward shuffle when advancing to narrow the shooting angle.
- Maintain the ready position when you begin to advance off the goal line.
- As the distance to the ball decreases, begin to break your body down by shifting into a semicrouch position.
- Maintain balance and body control.
- Never expose the near-post area.
- Be aware of the positions of defending teammates.
- During practice and games, check your position after every shot to ensure that the shooting angle was effectively narrowed.

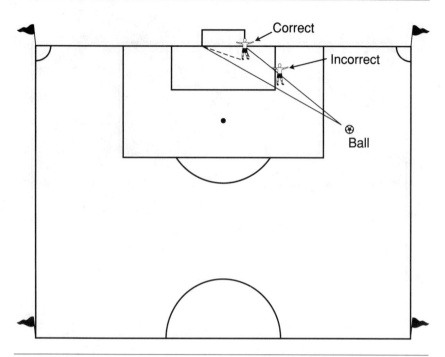

Figure 4.4   For a ball located in the flank area, you should move toward the ball, narrowing the shooting angle. In general, do not advance beyond the near post (the goalpost nearest the ball). Your position thus adequately narrows the shooting angle and allows recovery for a pass to the far-post area. Once it is obvious that the attacker is advancing toward the goal, you should move beyond the near post and confront the opponent.

Positioning for Crosses

Anticipate a cross whenever an opponent has possession of the ball near a touchline within range of the goal. Position yourself in the center of the goal area about 2 to 4 yards in front of the goal line. Use an open stance, with your feet pointing forward and your upper body at a three-quarters turn toward the ball (see Figure 4.5). In this position you are able to keep the ball in view and are also aware of opponents positioned within the penalty area. Do not square your shoulders to the server (see Figure 4.6), because your field of vision is limited in that position.

You should become increasingly concerned with protecting the near-post area of the goal as the ball moves inward from the flank. Be prepared to cut off the low hard cross driven across the goalmouth. At the same time you cannot neglect the possibility that the ball will be driven to the far post. Take into account several important factors when determining

Figures 4.5, 4.6 When you position yourself for crosses, your shoulders should be square to the field (Figure 4.5); keep your vision focused on the ball and allow a clear sight of opponents positioned within the penalty area. Facing the flank with your shoulders square to the ball (Figure 4.6) limits your vision of the field.

your best possible position in the goal area: (a) the position of the opponent's hips as she or he attempts to kick the ball, (b) the direction the ball is traveling in as the opponent approaches it, (c) the position of defending teammates, and (d) the ball's flight.

The position of the opponent's hips will dictate what he or she can do with the ball. If hips are square with the end line as the player prepares to kick the ball, then it is likely that the cross will be an outswinger curling away from the goal. You can then afford to position more centrally and farther off of the goal line. If the opponent's hips are angled toward the goal as she or he prepares to kick the ball, then anything is possible, including a shot to the near post. In that situation you should be more concerned with protecting the near-post area and move toward the front quarter of the goal.

If an opponent is chasing down a ball that is rolling diagonally away from the goal toward the touchline, then he or she will probably have to control it before crossing. A cross may be imminent if the ball is rolling toward the end line parallel to the touchline.

Always take into consideration the position of defending teammates. Is there a teammate near the ball who can prevent the cross? Can a teammate force the opponent to change direction before attempting a cross? Is a teammate positioned to intercept a crossed ball? Answers to these questions will enable you to position accordingly.

Finally, it is important that you assess the flight of the ball as it travels toward the goalmouth. What is its velocity and trajectory? Is the ball driven low and hard or high and lofted? Is it curving away from, or bending inward toward, the goal? You have only a few moments to analyze the situation and then respond appropriately.

Figure 4.7 provides general guidelines for goalkeeper positioning when the ball is located on the flank area. Exact positioning for each situation may vary slightly, depending upon individual strengths and weaknesses.

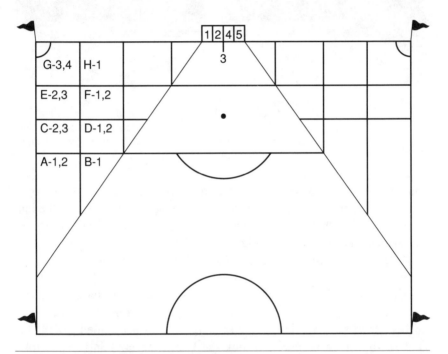

Figure 4.7 On the assumption that the ball is located on the left flank, areas where crosses are most likely to originate are lettered *A* through *H*. As the ball moves from one quadrant to another, you must adjust accordingly, anticipating the cross. The goal has been divided into sections. Depending on the location of the ball, you will be positioned in one of the five sections. For example, if the ball is in area A, you should position in sections 1 or 2 (noted as "A-1,2"). If an opponent with the ball is positioned in the flank near the end line (Area G), you should position in section 3 or 4, where you can react to a near-post cross while protecting the far-post area of the goal. Rarely, if ever, should you be positioned in the back of the goal (section 5); that would make you vulnerable to the near-post cross or shot. (If the ball is on the right flank, positioning is reversed.)

KEY ASPECTS OF PERFORMANCE

Positioning for Crosses

- Assume an open stance facing the field.
- Position according to the angle and distance of the ball from the goal.
- Anticipate the type of cross by looking for visual cues.
- Be aware of the positions of defending teammates.
- Analyze the ball's flight and adjust your position accordingly.
- Your first priority is to protect the near-post area.
- Attempt to cut off any cross before it travels across the goalmouth.
- Dominate the goal box!

Supporting the Defense— The Role of the Keeper/Sweeper

Be prepared to move forward out of the penalty area to protect the open space behind your defenders. Anticipate penetrating passes into that vulnerable space, and then move forward to beat opposing forwards to the ball. Base your decision on where to position according to the following general guidelines. Naturally these guidelines are subject to adjustment based upon your individual strengths and weaknesses (e.g., footwork, mobility, athleticism).

- Position 18 to 20 yards off of the goal line when the ball is in the opponent's end of the field.
- Position 8 to 12 yards off of the goal line when the ball is near midfield.
- Position 4 to 6 yards off of the goal line when the ball is in the defending third of the field but out of shooting range.

Determining the proper moment to rush forward to intercept the ball is difficult. There is little room for an error in judgment. Take into account the following factors when making your decision:

- The position of the ball

- Your speed off of the line
- The positions of defending teammates
- The positions and speed of opposing forwards

Communication

As goalkeeper, you have an excellent view of the field. From your vantage point you can communicate important information that will benefit teammates. Make your commands clear and concise to avoid any confusion.

Follow three basic guidelines when issuing verbal commands to teammates:

- Keep it simple—commands should be brief and to the point.
- Call early—provide teammates with sufficient time to respond.
- Call loudly—teammates won't usually have time to ask you to repeat the command.

Adopt a standard set of verbal signals to avoid any misunderstandings among teammates. Common goalkeeper commands can be grouped into the three following general categories.

Crucial Commands

The following commands are usually made in tense situations in and around the goal area. They must be made decisively and without hesitation.

- Call "Keeper!" to indicate that you intend to receive the ball.
- Call "Out!" or "Away!" when you want a defender to clear the ball out of the goal area.
- Call "Back!" to indicate that you want the ball passed back to you.

Organizational Commands

Issue the following commands when organizing the defense.

- Call "Close!" to instruct a defending teammate to reduce the space between her- or himself and the opponent with the ball.
- Call "Mark up!" to instruct a teammate to tightly mark an opponent.
- Call "Cover!" to instruct a teammate to provide support for the player who is challenging for the ball.
- Call "Balance!" to instruct teammates away from the ball to protect the space behind the defense.

- Call "Runner!" to inform teammates that an opponent is making a blind-side run behind the defense.

Attacking Commands

The following commands are generally used when your team is about to gain possession or has possession of the ball.

- Call "Man-on!" to inform a teammate that he or she is tightly marked from behind.
- Call "Turn!" to inform a teammate that she or he has sufficient space to turn with the ball.
- Call "Up or out!" to order teammates out of the goal or penalty area after the ball has been cleared.

In addition to verbal commands, you can use visual signals to communicate with teammates. For example, you can indicate where teammates should position or point out opponents who should be tightly marked. Visual signals are generally more difficult to interpret than verbal signals, however, so a combination of the two usually provides the best results.

Drills

General Instructions Applying to Drills

- Shout "Keeper!" when you are preparing to field the ball.
- Distribute the ball toward the opposite flank area after you receive a cross.
- Immediately smother any cross that is mishandled.
- Verbally communicate with teammates in drills that include defenders or opponents. Your commands should be loud and decisive.

Down-Up Drill

Equipment: 8 to 12 balls, 1 regulation-size goal

Organization: The goalkeeper assumes a sitting position 2 to 5 yards front and center of the goal line. The coach stands about 8 yards from the goal, facing the keeper, with the supply of balls. This drill is designed to help the keeper quickly get up from the ground into a ready position and set for a shot.

Procedure: On command the keeper jumps up, assumes the ready position, and catches a ball tossed by the coach. The keeper immediately returns to sitting position and repeats the drill. Continue for 60 seconds.

Variation: Same setup, except that the goalkeeper begins the drill by shuffling back and forth from post to post. On command the keeper drops to the ground in a push-up position, immediately jumps back up to a ready position, and catches a ball tossed by the coach. Repeat for 45 to 60 seconds.

Playing the Goalkeeper Arc

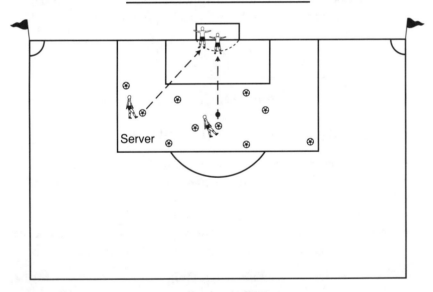

Equipment: 10 to 12 balls, 1 regulation-size goal

Organization: Place 10 to 12 balls at various distances and locations within the penalty area. One or more players (or coaches) are designated as servers. In this drill the goalkeeper should focus on proper footwork, stance, and movement along the goalkeeper arc.

Procedure: The server quickly moves from one ball to the next as if planning to shoot. The goalkeeper shuffles along the arc to maintain correct position between server, ball, and goal. (Note: The server does not actually shoot the ball.)

Variation #1:   Same setup, except that the server dribbles a ball laterally across the front edge of the penalty area while the keeper shuffles to maintain correct position between the ball and the goal. At her or his discretion the server shoots and the keeper saves. Repeat for 45 to 60 seconds.

Variation #2:   Same setup as in Variation #1, except that the speed of repetition is increased and two or three servers are used. The goalkeeper works at maximum intensity for 60 to 90 seconds.

Angle Action

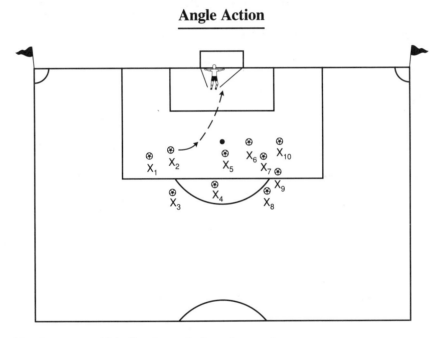

Equipment: 10 balls, 1 regulation-size goal

Organization: Position 6 to 10 players, each with a ball, across the dangerous scoring zone front and center of the goal. Players should be at least 15 yards from goal. The goalkeeper positions in the goal and concentrates on correct footwork, proper angle play, and quickly setting the feet for the shot.

Procedure: Each player, in turn, pushes the ball one or two steps toward goal and then shoots. The goalkeeper adjusts position according to the movement of the ball, sets in the ready position, and makes the save. Repeat until all servers have shot on goal.

Variation #1:   Same setup, except that each shooter is labeled with a number. The coach calls out numbers in random order; the player who is called quickly pushes the ball toward goal and shoots. The goalkeeper must immediately readjust position to align with the ball and then attempt to save. After each save, the keeper immediately prepares for the next shot.

Variation #2:   Shooters position facing the goal at a distance of about 40 yards. A server positions about 35 yards from the goal with the supply of balls. The server begins the exercise by playing a ball toward the goal; one of the shooters sprints forward, controls the ball, and shoots from a distance of about 20 yards. The goalkeeper attempts to save each shot.

Flank Play

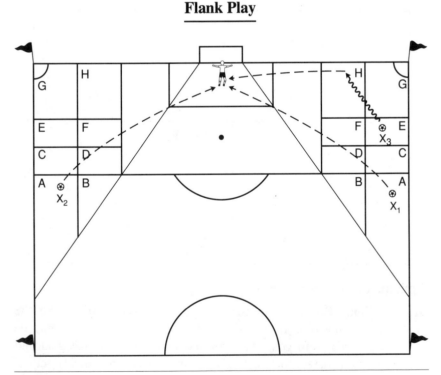

Figure 4.8

Equipment: 1 regulation-size goal, 28 cones or markers, 8 to 12 balls

Organization: Cones or flags are used to mark off grids as illustrated in Figure 4.8. Several players, each with a ball, are positioned in the marked grids (on both sides of the field). Cones divide the goal into 4 equal sections.

Procedure: Players alternate turns crossing a ball into the goal area from their respective grids on the flank. Alternate serves from one side of the field and then the other; for example, a serve from Grid A (Figure 4.8) on the right side of the field alternates with a serve from Grid A on the left side of the field. This continues until all of the balls have been served. The goalkeeper adjusts position depending upon the location of the grid from which the ball is served.

Variation #1:   Same setup, except that the coach calls out the name of the server from whom he or she wants the ball served. The goalkeeper immediately adjusts position in anticipation of the cross.

Variation #2:   Same setup as in Variation #1, except that, on the coach's command, the server dribbles into an adjacent grid and serves the ball from that position.

Variation #3:   Repeat variations #1 and #2, but with a defending team-mate positioned in front of the goalkeeper. The defender should vary her or his position and distance from the goal for each serve. The goalkeeper should communicate with the defender as he or she positions to field the crossed ball.

Variation #4:   Two or 3 defending teammates are added to Variation #3.

Variation #5:   Two or 3 attackers are added to Variation #4; they attempt to score off of the cross. The addition of attackers and defenders to the exercise creates a simulated game condition.

CHAPTER 5

Receiving Shots and Crosses

A goalkeeper must be able to handle shots arriving from different angles and traveling at high velocities. The ability to catch and hold the ball is of paramount importance, because rebounds or loose balls in the goal usually prove disastrous. Different receiving techniques are used for low, medium, and high balls.

The HEH Principle

HEH (hands, eyes, head) is a fundamental principle describing the proper way to align with the ball as it arrives. When possible, position your body in a direct line with the oncoming ball, providing a second barrier in the event the ball slips through your hands. Position your head directly behind your hands, with your vision focused on the ball. Hands, eyes, and head should all align with the ball (see Figure 5.1). Eliminate any unnecessary movement that may cause you to lose your focus. After receiving the ball, protect it by clutching it to your chest.

There will be times when it is not possible for you to position behind the ball. For example, you may have to quickly readjust position to save a deflected shot. In such cases attempt to save by whatever means possible.

Figure 5.1 The HEH principle: Align your hands, eyes, and head with the ball.

KEY ASPECTS OF PERFORMANCE

HEH Principle

- Place your hands, eyes, and head in a direct line.
- Keep your head steady, with your vision on the ball.
- "Watch" the ball directly into your hands.

The *W* Catch

The basic position of the hands when catching the ball is generally referred to as the *W*, or window (see Figure 5.2). Fingers are spread, with thumbs almost touching behind the ball. Employ the HEH principle as the ball approaches by looking through the window formed by your thumbs and index fingers. Fingers should be extended toward the ball and

Figure 5.2   The *W* catch: Keep thumbs together and palms on the sides of the ball.

slightly cupped. Receive the ball on your fingertips to help cushion the impact.

KEY ASPECTS OF PERFORMANCE

The *W* Catch

- Use the *W* hand position when catching any ball arriving above waist height.
- Thumbs almost touch, with palms on the sides of the ball.
- The ball first contacts your fingertips.
- Withdraw your hands toward your chest upon ball contact to cushion the impact.
- Develop "silent hands"—you should not hear a loud slap as the ball contacts your hands.
- Employ the HEH principle when using the *W* catch.

Receiving a Ground Ball

Figure 5.3 Use the standing save to receive a ball rolling directly at you. Use a shuffle movement to move sideways, positioning your body between the ball and the goal. Then bend at the waist, allow the ball to roll onto your wrists and forearms, clutch the ball to your chest, and return to a standing position.

The Standing Save

A ball rolling directly at you should be received from a standing position using the "scoop" technique (see Figure 5.3). As the ball arrives, bend forward at the waist with your legs straight and your feet a few inches apart. Extend your arms downward with palms forward and slightly cupped. Your fingertips should almost touch the ground. Position your forearms parallel with one another. Do not actually catch a rolling ball. Rather, allow the ball to roll up onto your wrists and forearms before clutching it to your chest.

On occasion you may go down on one knee to receive a ball rolling directly at you. However, it is recommended that you remain standing, for two primary reasons: (a) By dropping to one knee, you limit your ability to readjust your position if the ball takes a bad bounce; and (b) you can distribute the ball more quickly and efficiently from the standing position.

KEY ASPECTS OF PERFORMANCE

Standing Save

- Use this technique to receive a ball rolling directly at you.
- Keep your legs straight, with your feet a few inches apart.
- Bend forward at the waist in preparation to collect the ball.
- Allow the ball to roll onto your wrists and forearms, then secure it to your chest using the scoop technique.
- Keep your forearms parallel as you receive the ball.
- Provide a cushion by withdrawing your body slightly on ball impact.

Figure 5.4 Making the tweener save involves dropping to one knee, bending forward, and allowing the ball to roll up onto your wrists and forearms.

The Tweener Save

A low hard shot to either side of you is generally referred to as a "tweener." The ball is just far enough away to make the standing save impossible but not so distant as to require a diving save. To field the tweener you should quickly move laterally across the goal. Extend your lead foot, with the leg flexed at the knee. Kneel on the trailing leg, and align it parallel to the goal line. The open space between the trailing knee and the heel of the lead foot should be only a few inches—too small a space for a misplayed ball to skip through. Bend your upper body forward, with your head and shoulders square to the ball. Allow the ball to roll up onto your wrists and forearms before clutching it to your chest (see Figure 5.4). From this position you can quickly stand and distribute the ball.

KEY ASPECTS OF PERFORMANCE

Tweener Save

- Use the tweener save to field a ball rolling to either side of you.
- Position your trailing leg parallel to the goal line.
- Position the knee of your trailing leg a few inches from the heel of your lead foot.
- Position your shoulders and upper body square to the ball.
- Scoop the ball into your arms.
- Secure the ball to your chest and hop to your feet.

Figure 5.5   The forward vault can be used when saving a low, hard shot. Vault forward to meet the ball, extending your arms and hands underneath the ball. Then fall forward on your forearms and trap the ball between your chest and forearms.

The Forward Vault: Saving a Low Hard Shot

The conventional standing save is not appropriate for a low, powerfully driven shot aimed directly at you or for a shot that skips a yard or two in front of your feet. This is especially true when you are playing on a slick field surface where the ball accelerates upon hitting standing water or wet grass. In this situation use a different receiving technique to compensate for the added velocity of such shots (see Figure 5.5). From the ready position, bend forward at your waist, flex your knees, and vault forward toward the oncoming ball. Extend your arms and hands underneath the ball with palms facing up. The ball should first contact your wrists or forearms, not your hands. As the ball arrives, fall forward on your forearms and trap it between your chest and forearms. Your legs should be slightly spread and extended behind you for balance.

Figure 5.6   The forward vault also is used when smothering a loose ball. Vault out and forcefully pin the ball to the ground, with your palms covering the top and sides of the ball.

The Forward Vault: Smothering a Loose Ball

Loose balls in the goal area must be immediately covered, or smothered (see Figure 5.6). This situation may occur immediately after a shot has been deflected or when a cross has been misplayed. To smother a still or slowly rolling ball, vault forward with your palms facing down and forcefully pin the ball to the ground. Once the ball is secure, clutch it against your chest.

Figures 5.7, 5.8   When using the forward vault to collect a through ball, move forward and scoop the ball with your palms and forearms (Figure 5.7). Complete the forward motion by vaulting to the side of the onrushing opponent (Figure 5.8).

The Forward Vault: Collecting a Through Ball

A ball that has been played through the defense into the penalty area poses a special problem for the goalkeeper. This is a potentially dangerous situation, because one or more opponents may be rushing to get to the ball before you do. To avoid injury, quickly move forward, bend at the waist, and scoop up the ball between your forearms and chest. As you scoop the ball, vault forward and to the side of an onrushing opponent to avoid a collision (see Figures 5.7 and 5.8).

KEY ASPECTS OF PERFORMANCE

Forward Vault

- Use the forward vault to receive a low hard shot traveling directly at you, to smother a loose ball in the goal area, or to collect a through ball.
- To collect a low skipping shot aimed directly at you, bend at the waist and vault forward as your hands and forearms slip underneath the ball.
- When you smother a loose ball, forcefully pin it to the ground.
- When you scoop up a through ball, avoid colliding with an onrushing opponent by vaulting to the side of and past the opponent.
- Land on your forearms when vaulting forward.

Receiving a Medium-Height Ball

A medium-height ball is one that arrives between your ankles and midsection. Receive a medium-height ball using a technique similar to that employed when fielding a rolling ball (see Figure 5.9). Position your

Figure 5.9   Use the "scoop" technique when receiving a medium-height ball. Allow the ball to contact your wrists first, with your palms underneath and your upper body bent forward over the ball. Then clutch the ball to your chest.

body behind the ball with your legs a few inches apart. Bend your upper trunk forward with arms extended downward. Do not attempt to catch the ball. Rather, allow it to first contact your wrists and roll onto your forearms, and then clutch it against your chest as in Figure 5.10.

To receive a ball arriving at waist height, bend forward at your waist with your forearms parallel to one another and extended downward (see Figure 5.10). Jump backward a few inches as the ball arrives, to absorb the impact. Do not stand on the goal line when making the save, because by jumping backward to cushion the shot, you may inadvertently carry the ball over the goal line.

Figure 5.10 When receiving a medium-height ball, jump slightly backward, cushioning the impact of a hard shot.

KEY ASPECTS OF PERFORMANCE

Medium-Height Balls

- Allow the ball to contact your wrists and forearms before you clutch it against your chest.
- Lean forward over the ball as it arrives.
- Position your forearms parallel to one another.
- Stand with your feet several inches apart and your legs slightly flexed at the knees.
- Withdraw your body as the ball arrives, to cushion the impact.

Receiving a Chest-High or Head-High Ball

When you receive a chest- or head-high ball, the position of your hands will differ from that used for medium-height or rolling balls. Your fingers should be spread and extended toward the oncoming ball, with palms facing forward. The thumbs of both hands should almost touch in a *W* position. Extend your arms with forearms parallel. Slightly flex your elbows. Receive the ball on your fingertips, and then immediately draw in your arms to cushion the impact (see Figure 5.11). If the ball is powerfully driven, make sure your palms and fingers contact the upper half of the ball rather than the lower half. With your hands in that position, the ball will not skim off your fingertips into the goal. Once the ball is secured, clutch it to your chest.

Figure 5.11   Use the HEH principle when receiving a head-high ball.

KEY ASPECTS OF PERFORMANCE

Chest- and Head-High Balls

- Position your hands in the *W*.
- Employ the HEH principle.
- Extend your arms toward the ball with flexion at the elbows.
- Position your forearms parallel to one another.
- Align your palms with the top half of the ball.
- Catch the ball on your fingertips.
- Withdraw your hands and arms to cushion the impact.

Receiving a High Ball

Receiving and holding a high crossed ball is often the goalkeeper's greatest challenge. Success depends upon proper balance, precise timing, and good judgment. Always attempt to catch the ball at the highest possible point of your jump. Use a one-leg takeoff to generate maximum upward momentum (see Figure 5.12). The jumping movement looks similar to that used when shooting a lay-up in basketball.

Figures 5.12, 5.13   Use a one-leg takeoff with your arms extended up to catch the ball at the highest point possible.

It is essential that you jump off of the correct foot. Face the ball, take a step or two forward, and thrust the outside leg (toward the field) up. With your leg in this position you are protected from an onrushing opponent's attempt to head the ball. Your inside leg (nearest the goal) should remain straight to provide balance and also to serve as a stabilizing point when you return to the ground.

Your arms and takeoff leg should be thrust upward in one fluid motion. Point the knee of the takeoff leg in the direction of the ball to ensure that your shoulders are square with the ball. Position your hands in the W when fielding a ball that is driven with great velocity into the goal area (see Figure 5.13). Your hands can be spread slightly farther apart when fielding a softer, lofted ball. In both cases it is essential that you watch the ball directly into your hands. Once the ball has been received, secure it against your chest.

The goalkeeper must make two critical decisions when preparing to field a crossed ball—when to move toward the ball and when to jump up.

The most common mistake of inexperienced keepers is to step forward to meet the ball too soon or leave the ground too soon. To choose the correct course of action, you must quickly analyze the situation. What is the trajectory of the ball—is it rising or beginning to descend? What is its velocity? Is the ball swerving away from or into the goal area? Are there opponents who may beat you to the ball? Once you decide to move toward the ball, you must do so with speed and confidence. Take the shortest route to the spot where you will jump to intercept the ball. Try to time your run so as not to get to the takeoff spot too soon. You should be moving toward the ball as you jump up.

KEY ASPECTS OF PERFORMANCE

High Balls

- Square your shoulders with the flight of the ball.
- Generate momentum toward the ball in preparation to jump ("Come late, come hard!").
- Thrust your arms and outside leg up in one fluid motion when using the one-leg takeoff.
- Flex your outside leg (the one closest to the playing field) for protection.
- Extend your inside leg (the one closest to the goal line) to provide balance and stability in the event of a collision.
- Position your hands in the *W*.
- Receive crosses and lofted balls at the highest possible point.

Drills

The following drills are designed to improve your catching skills and to assist you in receiving ground and air balls. All exercises should be clearly explained and demonstrated to you before you practice them. It is important that you do sufficient repetitions until you have mastered the movement. Most exercises are organized to simulate conditions that occur in and around the goal area and may be adapted to suit your own needs and abilities.

Catching Exercises: *W* and HEH

Bouncing Through the Legs

Equipment: 1 ball per goalkeeper

Organization: The goalkeeper stands with legs spread, holding a ball with hands in the *W* position.

Procedure: Using two hands, the goalkeeper bounces the ball in a figure-eight position around the body and catches each rebound with hands in the *W* position.

Variation: Using two hands, the goalkeeper bounces the ball between the legs, turns at the waist, and catches it behind the body using the *W*. The keeper then bounces the ball back through the legs and catches it in front of the body, using the *W*. Repeat 30 times.

Bouncing Off the Board

Equipment: 1 ball per goalkeeper, a kickboard or wall

Organization: The goalkeeper stands with a ball, facing a kickboard or solid wall at a distance of about 5 to 8 yards

Procedure: The goalkeeper throws the ball hard off of the wall or kickboard, and receives the rebound using the HEH principle with hands in the *W* position.

Variation #1:   The goalkeeper sits facing a kickwall at a distance of about 5 yards with legs extended in a *V* position, throws the ball off the wall, and catches the rebound.

Variation #2:   The goalkeeper stands facing a kickboard or wall at a distance of 5 yards. A server positions 3 yards behind the goalkeeper. The server tosses a ball past the keeper and off of the wall; the goalkeeper reacts to the ball as it rebounds off of the board, and receives it using the *W* catch and HEH.

Pingers

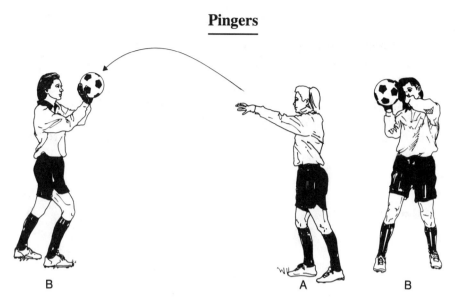

B   A   B

Equipment: 1 ball

Organization: Two goalkeepers (A and B) face one another, 3 yards apart.

Procedure: Goalkeeper A tosses a ball to the right or left of B, who takes a step sideways and receives the ball. Player B then serves the ball to A, who receives in a similar manner. All shots must be received using the *W* catch and HEH. Repeat 20 times each.

Variation: Two goalkeepers volley a ball back and forth at a distance of 8 to 10 yards.

Receiving Ground Balls

The Standing Save

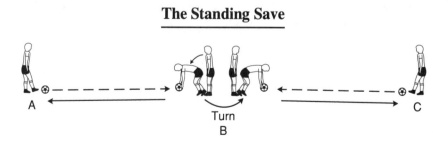

A   Turn   C
                            B

Equipment: 3 balls, 1 regulation-size goal

Organization: Three goalkeepers (A, B, and C) position in a straight line. A and C, each with a ball, face one other 8 yards apart, while B positions midway between them.

Procedure: Goalkeeper A rolls a ball to B, who scoops, saves, and returns the ball to A. Keeper B immediately turns, scoops a rolling ball from C, and returns the ball. Continue for 30 seconds; keepers then rotate positions and repeat.

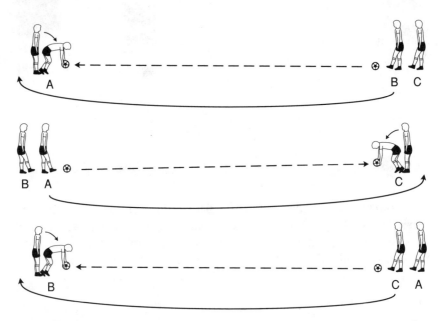

Variation #1:   Goalkeeper A faces two teammates (B and C) at a distance of 8 yards. B rolls a ball to A and immediately follows the ball by sprinting to A's position. Player A scoops and saves, rolls the ball to C, and sprints to C's position. Player C scoops and saves, rolls to B, and so on. Continue the drill for 60 seconds.

Variation #2:   One goalkeeper and three servers. The goalkeeper positions to defend a goal while the servers, each with a ball, face the goal along the 6-yard line. One server positions opposite each goalpost, while the third server stands opposite the center of the goal. On command the goalkeeper begins to shuffle back and forth along the goalkeeper arc. Each server, in turn, rolls a ball toward the keeper, who scoops and saves, then returns the ball to the server. Continue for 60 seconds.

Saving the Tweener Ball

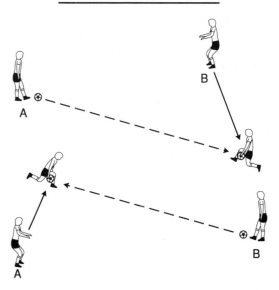

Equipment: 4 to 6 balls, 1 regulation-size goal

Organization: Two goalkeepers (A and B) face one another at a distance of 8 yards.

Procedure: Goalkeeper A rolls a ball to the left of B, who receives it using the tweener save. Keeper B returns the ball by rolling it to A's left. Keeper A kneels and saves, then returns the ball to B's right, and so on. Continue until each keeper has received 15 to 20 balls.

A   B

Variation: One goalkeeper and two servers. The goalkeeper positions near the right goalpost. Servers A and B stand on the 6-yard line, opposite each post. Server A begins by rolling a ball toward the center of the goal. The goalkeeper quickly shuffles across the goal, receives the ball using the tweener save, immediately returns the ball to the server, and continues across the goal until reaching the left goalpost. At that point Server B rolls a ball toward the center of the goal. The keeper shuffles sideways, receives the ball using the tweener save, and returns the ball to the server. Continue the exercise for 60 to 90 seconds.

Forward Vault for Low Hard Shots

A   B

Equipment: 1 ball

Organization: Goalkeepers A and B kneel facing one another at a distance of 5 yards.

Procedure: Goalkeeper A bounces a ball toward B, who vaults forward to meet the ball and receives it with palms facing up and forearms underneath the ball. Keeper B returns the ball to A in a similar manner. Continue until each keeper has fielded 15 to 20 shots.

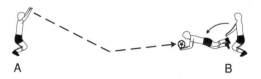

A   B

Variation #1:   Same setup, except that the goalkeepers start from a squat position.

Variation #2:   Goalkeepers A and B face one another in the ready position at a distance of 12 yards. Keeper A throws a low hard serve toward B's feet. B vaults forward to make the save and then serves a similar ball to A. The goalkeepers should vary the trajectory and velocity of serves.

Smothering Loose Balls

Equipment: 1 ball

Organization: Goalkeeper stands holding a ball with feet spread shoulder-width apart.

Procedure: Keeper rolls the ball through his or her legs, quickly turns, and then leaps backward to smother the ball by pinning it to the ground. Repeat at maximum speed for 40 seconds.

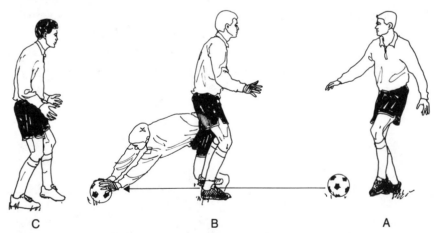

C   B   A

Variation: Goalkeepers A, B, and C position in a straight line. A and C are 8 yards apart, with B midway between them. Keeper B faces A with feet shoulder-width apart. Keeper A rolls the ball through B's legs, and B turns and vaults out to smother the ball. B then gives the ball to C, who repeats the exercise by rolling the ball through B's legs. B turns, smothers the ball, and gives it to A. Continue the exercise for 40 seconds, then keepers rotate positions.

Collecting Through Balls

Equipment: 1 ball

Organization: Goalkeepers A, B, and C position in a straight line. A and C stand 12 yards apart, while B stands, with legs spread, midway between A and C.

Procedure: Goalkeeper A rolls a ball through B's legs; C quickly moves forward and uses the forward vault technique to collect the ball. Keeper C must vault to the side of B after making the save. Players return to their original positions, then C rolls the ball through B's legs, and A uses the forward vault to save. Continue for 40 seconds. Players then rotate positions.

Variation: A goalkeeper, a server, and a chaser. The server, with 4 to 6 balls, stands facing the goal at a distance of 30 yards. The chaser stands beside the server. The server pushes a slowly paced ball toward the penalty area; the chaser waits a moment and then sprints to catch up to the ball. The goalkeeper sprints forward off of the goal line, leans forward, scoops the ball, and then vaults forward and to the side of the onrushing chaser. (Note: The chaser should let the goalkeeper win the race to the ball).

Receiving Air Balls

Waist-High Balls

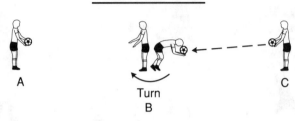

A

Turn
B

C

Equipment: 3 balls, 1 regulation-size goal

Organization: Same as for Standing Save drill on pages 61-63.

Procedure: Same as for Standing Save drill, except that instead of receiving a rolling ball, the keeper receives a waist-high ball. Servers should toss the ball using an underhand throwing motion.

Variation #1: Same format as in Variation #1 of the Standing Save drill, except that instead of a rolling ball, a waist-high ball is served. Servers should toss the ball using an underhand throwing motion.

Variation #2: Three servers, each with a ball, position about 10 yards from the goal (see page 63 for setup). One server is opposite each goalpost, while the third positions opposite the center of the goal. The goalkeeper slowly shuffles from post to post along the goalkeeper arc. Servers alternate volleying the ball out of their hands directly at the keeper's waist. The goalkeeper saves each shot and returns the ball to the server. Repeat for 60 seconds.

Chest- and Head-High Balls

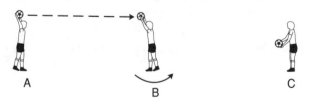

A

B

C

Equipment: 2 balls

Organization: Goalkeepers A, B, and C position in a straight line. A and C, each with a ball, face one another at a distance of 10 yards, with B midway between them.

Procedure: Keeper A tosses a chest- or head-high ball to B, who receives using the proper technique. B returns the ball to A, immediately turns, and receives a ball tossed by C. Continue for 60 seconds, after which players rotate positions and repeat the exercise.

Variation: Same setup, except that servers volley the ball out of their hands.

Receiving the High Ball

Equipment: 1 ball

Organization: Keeper stands holding the ball

Procedure: The goalkeeper tosses a ball high into the air, then uses a one-leg takeoff to jump up and catch the ball at the highest point possible.

Variation #1:   Repeat the Standing Save drill on pages 61-63 except that serves are high lofted balls.

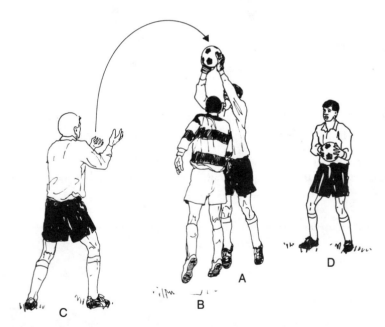

Variation #2:   Four goalkeepers (A, B, C, and D). Keepers C and D, each with a ball, face one another at a distance of 12 to 15 yards; Keepers A and B stand together midway between C and D. Keeper C serves a high lofted ball toward Keeper A, who must jump up and over B to catch the ball. After receiving the ball, A returns it to C. A and B then turn to face D, who serves a high lofted ball toward B. B jumps up and over A, catches the ball, and returns it to D. Repeat the exercise for 60 to 90 seconds, with A and B alternating turns receiving the high lofted ball. A and B then become servers, and C and D move to the center to receive high lofted balls.

High-Ball Pressure Training

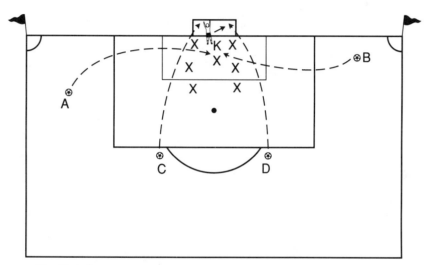

X = Passive opponents

Equipment: 10 to 12 balls, 1 regulation-size goal

Organization: The goalkeeper positions in the goal. Four servers (A, B, C, and D) position just outside of the penalty box, A and B on the flanks and C and D more centrally.

Procedure: Starting with Server A, the servers in turn toss, volley, or chip a high ball into the penalty area. The goalkeeper moves toward the ball, jumps up using the correct takeoff leg, and catches the ball at the highest point possible. After each save the keeper repositions in the goal. Servers should vary the type of service, including inswingers, outswingers, high lofted balls, and hard-driven crosses.

Variation: Same setup, except that several passive opponents position in the penalty area to impede the goalkeeper's path to the ball.

Functional High-Ball Training

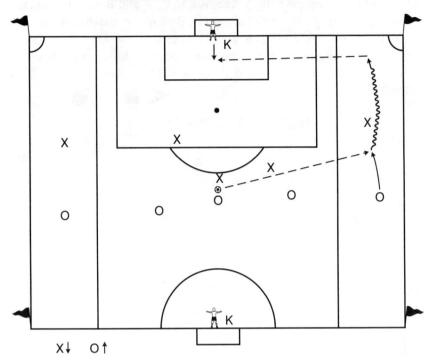

X↓   O↑

Equipment: 2 regulation-size goals (one should be portable), 6 to 8 balls, 6 to 12 cones or markers

Organization: Play 5-on-5 on a half field with a regulation-size goal on each end line. A goalkeeper positions to defend each goal. Cones or flags mark off a 10-yard-wide lane on each flank. Each team positions 1 player in each flank area.

Procedure: Teams play 3-on-3 in the central portion of the field between the lanes. The flank players are unopposed in their lanes. When flank players receive the ball from a teammate or their goalkeeper, they must dribble to the end line and cross the ball into the goal area. Teammates in the central zone try to score off of the crosses, while defending players try to prevent the score. If the goalkeeper receives a crossed ball or saves a shot taken by a central player, she or he must immediately distribute the ball to the teammate positioned in the opposite flank area. Because the primary objective of this exercise is goalkeeper training, it is essential that most of the crosses be placed within the keeper's range.

CHAPTER 6

The Uncatchable High Ball

In some instances you may not be confident that you can catch a high ball driven into the goal area. For example, the ball may be dipping or swerving, it may be a wet or windy day, or a collision with an opponent may be imminent. When in doubt, always choose safety first rather than risk a costly error. Instead of trying to catch the ball, box it away from the goal area.

Boxing

Boxing, also referred to as punching, is the technique used to clear a high ball out of the goal area under extreme pressure or in adverse weather conditions. As a general rule, if one or more of the following conditions are present, you should box rather than catch the ball.

- There is a likelihood of a strong physical challenge from an opponent.
- The penalty area is crowded, and the path to the ball is blocked.
- You are knocked off balance when you jump up to receive the ball.

- The ball is curving away from your reach, and you are unsure of holding it.
- Weather conditions are poor (bad footing, wet or snow-covered field, slick and slippery ball, etc.).
- Other factors raise doubts about your ability to hold the ball.

Two-Fisted Box Technique

Use the two-fisted box in situations where you can square your shoulders with, and move directly toward, the oncoming ball. Attempt to box the ball high, far, and wide toward a flank area. Achieving height on the clearance will give teammates extra moments to organize and regroup. Boxing the ball as far as possible from the goal area reduces the likelihood of an immediate scoring attempt. Boxing the ball toward the flank area removes it from the most dangerous scoring zone, front and center of the goal. Never box the ball down toward the ground within the penalty area, where an opponent may be positioned to drive it into the goal.

You must use correct boxing technique to generate maximum height and distance on the clearance. In preparation to box, form two solid fists with your hands together (see Figure 6.1). Your wrists should be firm and your hands positioned with thumbs on top. Your elbows should be flexed and held tightly against your sides. To generate maximum power, quickly extend your arms to meet the ball. The arm thrust must be a compact, explosive-type movement. Fists contact the ball just below its center. Use the one-leg takeoff when you jump up and over opponents to

Figure 6.1   When positioning your hands for the two-fisted box, form two solid fists with knuckles together, providing a flat surface. Your wrists must be locked and your hands positioned so that your thumbs are on top. Tuck your elbows to the sides.

Figure 6.2   Use a one-leg takeoff to jump when you use the two-fisted boxing technique. Your outside leg (the one nearest the playing field) should be thrust upward and your fists driven through the ball with a compact, explosive extension of your arms.

box the ball. Contact the ball at the highest point of your jump (see Figure 6.2).

KEY ASPECTS OF PERFORMANCE

Two-Fisted Box

- Use this technique to box a high ball traveling directly at you.
- Box the ball high, far, and wide of the goal.
- Keep your fists tightly clenched, elbows tight to sides, and wrists locked.
- Extend your arms with a short, powerful motion as your fists are driven through the ball.

One-Fisted Box Technique

Use the one-fisted box to continue the flight of a crossed ball in the same direction as it is traveling in. To do so, box the ball across your body (see Figure 6.3). For example, a ball crossed from the left flank should be boxed with the right hand to continue its flight toward the opposite

Figure 6.3   The one-fisted boxing technique is most appropriate when continuing the flight of the ball in the same direction as its original trajectory.

touchline. A short, powerful extension of the arm across your body provides the greatest degree of control. Avoid a wide, looping arm swing.

The one-fisted box technique is also appropriate when you are caught off of the goal line with a high ball dropping behind you. In that situation it is best to box the ball over the crossbar and out of play. Keep the ball in sight, quickly take a drop step with the foot farthest from the ball, and then box the ball with a short, compact extension of your opposite arm. Keep in mind that you should box the ball over the bar only if you are unsure of catching it. Through proper footwork and correct anticipation you should be able to catch most high balls.

Follow this simple rule to box a ball that is dropping behind you:

Drop-step left and box across your body with your right hand, for a ball that is dropping over your left shoulder; drop-step right and box across your body with your left hand, for a ball dropping over your right shoulder.

KEY ASPECTS OF PERFORMANCE

One-Fisted Box

- Use the one-fisted technique to box a high ball crossed from the flank or to box a ball that is dropping behind you.
- When boxing a crossed ball, continue its flight toward the opposite touchline.
- Take a drop step and bring the opposite arm and fist across your body.
- Box the ball with a short, compact extension of your arm.
- Focus your vision on the ball throughout your boxing motion.

Open-Palm Technique

You can also use your open palm to handle a ball dipping over your head or a ball that is dropping just beneath the crossbar. Rather than boxing the ball, guide the ball over the crossbar with your open hand or hands. This is generally referred to as "turning" the ball over the bar. You may use one or both hands to turn the ball, depending upon the shot.

Use the two-hand technique to handle a powerful shot coming directly toward you. Position your hands so that the palms face forward and are angled slightly back from the vertical. Contact the ball just beneath its center, with your wrists firmly positioned. Extend your arms diagonally upward upon ball contact, just enough to alter the flight of the ball over the bar.

Use one hand to turn a ball that is dropping behind you near the crossbar. The technique is similar to the one-fisted box. Judge the flight of the ball, quickly adjust to it, and then take a drop step with the foot farthest from the ball. For example, take the drop step with your left foot if the ball is crossed from your right side and is dropping over your left shoulder. Your right arm and hand come across your body to turn the ball over the bar (see Figure 6.4). The reverse holds true on a ball dropping over your right shoulder. Use the nonpalming arm and hand for balance and also to "feel" for the crossbar. Touching the bar as you prepare to turn the ball will give you an idea of your position in relation to the goal. Rotate your body to face the ground immediately after turning the ball.

Figure 6.4   The ball can be turned over the bar with the open palm. As the ball approaches, position yourself sideways-on, focusing your vision on the ball. Use your palm and fingers to turn the ball over the bar.

As you fall, your arms and hands should contact the ground first. Tuck your shoulder, and roll to cushion the impact.

KEY ASPECTS OF PERFORMANCE

Open Palm

- Use the open palm to turn a ball that is dropping behind you over the crossbar.
- Your palm contacts the lower half of the ball and gently lifts the ball over the bar.
- Use a drop step right and turn the ball with your left hand, for a ball dropping over your right shoulder. Reverse the technique for a ball dropping over your left shoulder.
- Keep the ball in sight at all times.

Drills

The following drills are designed to improve your two- and one-fisted boxing and open palm techniques. All exercises should be clearly explained and demonstrated to you before you practice them. It is important that you do sufficient repetitions until you have mastered the movement. Most exercises are organized to simulate conditions that occur in and around the goal area and may be adapted to suit your own needs and abilities.

Two-Fisted Boxing

Fundamental Two-Fisted Boxing

C   B   A

Equipment: 2 to 4 balls

Organization: Goalkeepers A, B, and C position 5 yards apart in a straight line. Goalkeeper C (on the end) kneels facing B, who is in the middle. (Goalkeeper A is 5 yards behind B.)

Procedure: Keeper B tosses a lofted ball toward C, who boxes the ball over B to A. Keepers immediately rotate positions and repeat. Keepers continue the exercise until each has boxed 20 tossed balls.

Variation: Same setup, except that the goalkeeper who is boxing the ball begins in a squat position, then progresses to a standing position. Increase the distance between keepers to 10 yards.

Boxing Over the Opponent

Equipment: 2 to 4 balls

Organization: Two pairs of goalkeepers (A-B and C-D) participate in this exercise. Keepers A and B stand together midway between C and D, who stand 12 yards apart.

Procedure: Keeper C tosses a lofted ball toward A and B. A jumps up and over B and boxes the ball back to C. A and B then turn to face D. D serves a ball to B, who jumps over A and boxes the ball back to D. A and B alternate boxing the ball for 60 seconds, then switch positions with C and D.

One-Fisted Boxing

Fundamental One-Fisted Boxing

Equipment: 2 to 4 balls

Organization: One goalkeeper kneels sideways between 2 servers (A and B), who stand facing one another 12 yards apart.

Procedure: Server A tosses a lofted ball toward the keeper, who continues the flight of the ball by boxing it across his or her body to B. Server B then serves the ball so that the keeper must use the opposite arm to box the ball to A. The goalkeeper boxes 15 tosses with each hand.

Variation: Same setup, except that the goalkeeper begins in a squat position, then progresses to a standing (ready) position. Increase the distance of the serves to 15 to 20 yards.

Boxing a Crossed Ball

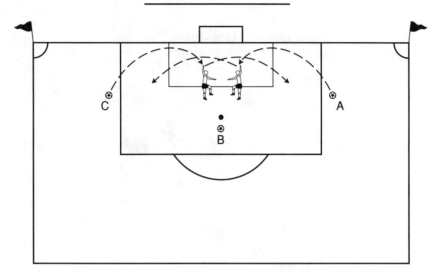

Equipment: 8 to 10 balls, 1 regulation-size goal

Organization: Three servers position around the penalty area. Servers A and C position on each flank, while Server B positions near the penalty spot. The goalkeeper positions in the goal.

Procedure: Server A on the right flank drives a cross into the goal area; the goalkeeper must box with the left hand to continue the flight of the ball toward the opposite flank. Server C then crosses a ball from the left flank, which the keeper boxes with the right hand to continue the ball's flight to the right flank. After boxing, the goalkeeper immediately advances toward Server B, who tosses a ball toward the goal that will drop near the crossbar. The keeper quickly retreats toward the goal and uses proper arm action to box the ball over the bar. The keeper performs three repetitions of the circuit and then switches with one of the servers.

The Open Palm

Fundamental Palming Technique

Equipment: 2 to 4 balls

Organization: Goalkeepers A and C face one another 10 yards apart. Goalkeeper B stands midway between them facing A.

Procedure: Goalkeeper A serves a high ball over B's right shoulder; B takes a drop step with the right foot and uses the open palm of the left hand to direct the ball to C. Keeper C then serves a ball over B's left shoulder; B takes a drop step with the left foot and uses the open palm of the right hand to direct the ball to A. Goalkeeper B turns 10 serves with each hand, then switches positions with a server.

Turning Over the Bar

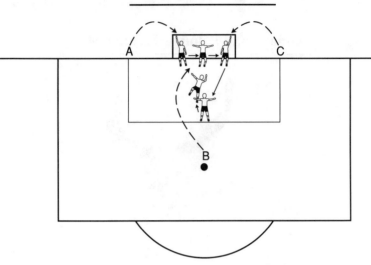

Equipment: 6 to 12 balls, 1 regulation-size goal

Organization: Servers A and C position at the intersections of the goal area and the end line. Server B stands on the penalty spot. The goalkeeper positions at the far post of the goal in relation to Server A, who is on the right side of the goal.

Procedure: Server A tosses a high ball into the goal area near the crossbar. The goalkeeper must move to the ball and turn it safely out of play with the open palm. After turning the ball over the bar, the keeper continues to shuffle across the goal, touches the post, and turns to receive a high serve from C, who is positioned on the left side of the goal box. After turning that ball over the bar, the keeper shuffles forward toward Server B, who tosses a high ball toward the crossbar. The goalkeeper must immediately take a drop step, position accordingly, and turn the ball over the bar. Repeat the sequence several times.

Functional Exercises for Uncatchable High Balls

Repeat the drills High-Ball Pressure Training and Functional High-Ball Training from chapter 5 (pages 71, 72). Instead of catching the ball, however, the keeper should use the appropriate boxing or turning technique.

7

The Diving Save

One of the most thrilling sights in soccer is a goalkeeper flying through the air to save a difficult shot. Diving skills are as important as they are exciting to watch. Proper execution requires anticipation, correct technique, precise timing, and courage. Even though they're a spectator favorite, diving skills should be used only when needed and never merely for show. Mistakes are likely to occur when sound goalkeeping tactics are replaced by needless acrobatic and attention-seeking antics.

Diving for Ground Balls

The low hard shot to the side, often referred to as the "grasscutter," is a difficult challenge for the keeper. You must coordinate the movement of your legs and upper body to vault toward the spot where the ball can be intercepted.

When you dive to save ground balls of *medium velocity*, two foot movements—the side shuffle and collapse step—are particularly important. Use the side shuffle to close the distance to the ball, then use the collapse step to fall quickly and smoothly to the ground. Start the collapse step by pushing off with the foot nearest the ball. For example, push off your right foot when you are diving to the right (see Figures 7.1, 7.2, and 7.3).

Figures 7.1, 7.2, 7.3 A sequence of steps is used when diving for a ground ball traveling at medium velocity. Figure 7.1 shows the initial movement as you begin to go to the ground. Figure 7.2 demonstrates the collapse step with the foot nearest the ball, and Figure 7.3 illustrates pinning the ball to the ground.

The opposite leg and arm follow to generate added momentum in the direction of the dive. The greater the distance of the dive, the more you must emphasize the follow-through motion of the opposite leg and arm.

Employ the HEH (hands-eyes-head) principle to ensure proper position of your body behind the ball. Position your hands in a sideways version of the *W*, and receive the ball on your fingertips and palms. Place your lower hand directly behind the ball, with your elbow tucked (see Figure 7.4). The upper hand comes down hard on top of the ball, pinning it to the ground. Proper hand position will prevent you from rolling after making the save and also helps to secure the ball. Once the ball is pinned to the ground, you should pull it in to your chest.

To save a ball traveling with *great velocity*, you may not have time to shuffle. Immediately take a power step with the foot nearest the ball and push off. The opposite arm and leg follow to generate momentum in the direction of the dive. Fully extend your lower arm because that hand

Figure 7.4 In correct diving technique, you land on your side. Place one hand behind the ball, and the other on top, pinning the ball to the ground.

should contact the ball first. The opposite (upper) hand comes down on top of the ball to pin it to the ground.

In correct diving technique, you contact the ground on your side. Do not dive on your stomach, because in that position (a) you provide less of an obstacle, (b) it is impossible to use the HEH principle, (c) your back and kidneys are exposed to overly aggressive opponents attempting to kick the ball, and (d) there is greater likelihood that you will land on top of the ball, which may cause internal injury.

When you are diving to save a ground ball, remember the basic rule of goalkeeping: When in doubt, always choose safety first. If you are unsure of holding the ball, parry it wide of the goal with the open palm of your lower hand (see Figure 7.5). Angle your hand slightly back, with the wrist firm. Contact the inside half of the ball with your open palm to deflect the ball wide of the goal. Do not position your open palm directly behind the ball, because that may cause the ball to rebound in front of the goal.

Figure 7.5   Use the open palm of your lower hand when you deflect a low shot wide of the goal.

Diving for Air Balls

The basic techniques used when diving for low shots also apply for shots traveling above ground. Proper footwork is essential to generate maximum momentum in the direction of the dive. To save a ball to your immediate side, use a quick side shuffle followed by a collapse step. Use a power step when you must vault through the air to save. Take a short, sideways step with the foot nearest the ball, pointing your toe in the direction of the dive. Slight flexion of your knee will aid your balance and body control. Push off with the foot nearest the ball while simultaneously vaulting the opposite leg upward. The opposite arm should follow in a powerful, whiplike motion upward and behind your head (see Figure 7.6). Do not project your arm across your body; that movement will tend to pull your body down toward the ground and shorten your dive. Extend your body parallel to the ground as your hands contact the ball.

Figure 7.6   When you dive to save a shot traveling above ground, take a power step in the direction of the ball, use your opposite arm and leg to vault sideways, catch the ball, and land with the ball contacting the ground first.

After you catch the ball, your immediate concern is to land properly. The ball should contact the ground first to partially cushion your fall, followed by your forearm, shoulder, hip, and leg, in that order. It is important that you tuck your elbow when landing. Failure to do so may cause you to lose your grip on the ball, injure your elbow, or both. Pin the ball to the ground with your legs positioned in a sideways *V*. Proper leg position ensures greater coverage of the goal in case the ball is jarred loose. As always, protect the ball by pulling it to your chest.

Deflecting Air Balls: The Reaction Save

You may not have time to worry about correct footwork or coordinated body movement when saving a point-blank blast. In that situation a successful save may depend solely on instinct and immediate reaction. As the saying goes, he who hesitates is lost. Attempt to box or deflect the shot rather than catch the ball. You can do so in three ways:

- The open palm can be used for both low and high shots.
- The flat surface of a closed fist can be used for high shots.
- The heel of the hand (with fist closed) can be used for low shots.

It is essential that you vault sideways and get parallel to the ground as quickly as possible (see Figure 7.7). Anticipation, quickness, and a bit of luck all play a part in the successful reaction save.

Figure 7.7 For the reaction save, use the open palm or heel of your lower hand and deflect the ball wide of the goal.

KEY ASPECTS OF PERFORMANCE

Diving to Save

- Practice diving in a soft area of the field or in a sawdust pit. Use a regulation-size goal whenever possible.
- Wear protective pads, particularly over your hips and elbows, when practicing diving skills.
- Begin in the ready position.
- Close the distance to the ball by shuffling your feet.
- Use the collapse step to save most ground balls.
- Use the power step to save most air balls.
- Push off with the foot nearest the ball.
- Use correct motion of your opposite arm and leg to generate momentum.
- Tuck your elbow when falling.
- Pin the ball to the ground—with one hand on top and one behind.
- Hit the ground in the following sequence: ball, forearm, shoulder, hip, legs.
- Contact the ground on your side.
- Pull the ball to your chest once you have pinned it to the ground.
- Choose safety first; if you are unsure of holding the ball, box or deflect it wide of the goal.
- Use your upper hand to deflect balls above your waist; use your lower hand to deflect balls below your waist.

Drills

All exercises should start slowly. The goalkeeper should progress to more intense training only after she or he has developed sufficient confidence and proficiency in diving skills.

Catching Ground Balls

Fundamental Diving

Equipment: 2 balls

Organization: Two goalkeepers kneel facing one another. Place a ball to the immediate right and left of each keeper.

Procedure: On command both keepers fall to their right and, using the HEH principle, pin the ball to the ground. Keepers return to a kneeling position and repeat the dive to the opposite side. Continue for 40 seconds, then rest, and repeat.

Variation #1:   Same setup, except that the goalkeepers begin from a squat position. The balls are positioned 3 to 4 yards to each side of the keepers. Emphasize motion of the opposite arm (the one farthest from the ball). The arm should be thrust up and behind the head to generate momentum in the direction of the dive.

Variation #2:   Same setup as in Variation #1, except that the goalkeepers begin from the ready position. The balls are positioned 4 to 6 yards to each side of the keepers. The goalkeepers take a collapse step before falling sideways to pin the ball to the ground.

Variation #3:   One goalkeeper and one server. The goalkeeper faces a server at a distance of 5 yards. The server rolls a ball 2 or 3 yards to the keeper's side; the keeper dives to save. The server alternates serving to the right and the left side of goalkeeper. Continue for 40 seconds, rest, and repeat.

Shuffle and Save

Equipment: 4 to 6 balls, 1 regulation-size goal

Organization: A server stands 8 yards front and center of the goal; the goalkeeper positions at the left goalpost, facing the server.

Procedure: The server rolls a ball toward the center of the goal. The goalkeeper shuffles sideways, uses the collapse step, and pins the ball to the ground, then immediately jumps up and continues to shuffle sideways to the right post. The server then rolls another ball toward the center of the goal. Continue for 40 seconds, rest, and repeat.

Variation: The server positions 8 yards front and center of the goal. The goalkeeper positions in the center of the goal. The server alternates rolling the ball to the right and the left of the keeper, who shuffles sideways, takes a collapse step, and pins the ball to ground. Continue for 40 seconds, rest, and repeat.

Deflecting Ground Balls

The Deflection Save

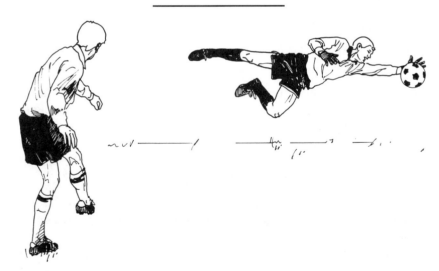

Equipment: 4 to 6 balls

Organization: Same as the Shuffle and Save drill, pages 92-93.

Procedure: Same as the Shuffle and Save drill, except that the server should increase the pace of the serve, forcing the keeper to deflect the ball past the post with the lower hand rather than catch it.

Catching Air Balls

Fundamental Flying

Equipment: 2 to 4 balls

Organization: The keeper assumes a squat position and faces a server positioned 4 to 6 yards away.

Procedure: The server tosses a ball to the keeper's side, forcing him or her to dive and save. The goalkeeper should concentrate on catching the ball and using proper motion of the opposite arm and leg to generate momentum in the direction of the dive. After each save, the keeper resumes the original position and then repeats the exercise to the opposite side. Continue for 40 seconds, rest, and repeat.

Variation: The keeper begins in the ready position, with the server positioned 6 yards away. The server tosses a ball to the side of the keeper so that she or he must take a short power step when diving to save. After each save the keeper quickly returns to the ready position in preparation for the next serve. The server alternates tossing to the right and the left. Continue for 40 seconds, rest, and repeat.

Power Flying

Equipment: 4 to 6 balls, 1 regulation-size goal, 2 to 4 cones or possibly an obstacle such as a bale of hay

Organization: An obstacle (ball, cone, kneeling teammate, bale of hay) is placed about 1 yard to the side of the keeper. A server is positioned opposite the goalkeeper, about 8 yards away.

Procedure: The server tosses a ball to the side of the keeper but within diving distance. The goalkeeper takes a power step and vaults over the obstacle to catch the ball. Emphasize proper landing to cushion the fall. Continue for 40 seconds, alternating dives to the right and the left.

Variation #1:   Same setup, except that the keeper positions 6 yards from the obstacle. To save, the keeper must shuffle sideways, take a power step, and dive over the obstacle.

Variation #2:   Same setup as the Shuffle and Save drill (pages 92-93), except that the ball is served through the air rather than on the ground and the dive is preceded by a side shuffle and power step.

Deflecting Air Balls

Deflecting Technique

Equipment: 2 to 4 balls

Organization: The goalkeeper begins in a squat position. A server holds a ball in each hand with arms outstretched facing the goalkeeper at a distance of 1 yard. A third player positions nearby to keep the server supplied with balls.

Procedure: The server tosses one of the balls to the keeper's side. The keeper must quickly react to deflect the ball with the open palm of the upper hand or by boxing. The server alternates tossing to the keeper's right and left. Continue for 40 seconds, rest, and repeat.

Variation: Same setup, except that the server tosses the ball to the ground, forcing the keeper to save with the lower hand. The save should be made with the open palm or the heel of the hand. Continue for 40 seconds, rest, and repeat.

Goalkeeper Competitions

Keeper vs. Keeper

Equipment: 6 to 8 balls, 2 regulation-size goals

Organization: Position 2 regulation goals 20 yards apart with a goal-keeper in each goal.

Procedure: One keeper holds a ball and is permitted to take four steps forward before attempting to shoot, volley, or throw the ball into the opposing goal. He or she is awarded 1 point for a goal scored. The defending goalkeeper can advance off of the goal line to narrow the angle and save. The defending goalkeeper is awarded 2 points for catching the ball and 1 point for deflecting it wide of the goal. Keepers alternate shooting at one another. Play to a predetermined number of points.

Variation: Same setup, except that a second player is added to each team as the designated "shooter." The goalkeeper distributes the ball to her or his teammate after each save. The shooter is permitted only two touches to control and shoot the ball at the opposite goal.

All vs. Keeper

Equipment: 2 to 4 balls, 1 regulation-size portable central goal (or cones or flags to represent a goal)

Organization: A regulation-size goal is positioned in the center of a 30-by-40-yard field. A neutral goalkeeper positions to defend the goal.

Procedure: Play 5-on-5 in the 30-by-40-yard area. Field players are permitted to score from either side of the central goal, so the goalkeeper must constantly readjust position in relation to the movement of the ball. Teams are awarded 1 point for each goal scored; the goalkeeper is awarded 1 point for each save. After each save the keeper distributes the ball to a corner of the playing area, and teams vie for possession.

Stopping the Breakaway

An opponent with the ball who has broken free of defenders and is approaching the goal presents a difficult challenge to the goalkeeper. Breakaways occur from different angles with players of different dribbling speeds and abilities. As a consequence, each breakaway situation is unique. Even so, the goalkeeper can apply to all breakaway situations several basic principles that will help shift the advantage to the goalkeeper.

Challenging the Dribbler

Once a dribbler penetrates the defense and is clear of all defenders, you must move forward to narrow the shooting angle to the goal. Begin in the ready position (see Figure 8.1), then shift into a semicrouch position as you advance toward the ball (see Figure 8.2). The nature of your challenge depends upon the speed and angle of the opponent's approach. Quickly move forward to challenge if the ball is well ahead of the dribbler and not under his or her immediate control. Advance more slowly and with greater control if the attacker has close possession of the ball. Angle your approach to the ball in an attempt to maneuver the opponent diagonally away from the goal so as to narrow the shooting angle. Do not allow

Figures 8.1, 8.2   When you challenge the dribbler in a breakaway situation, begin the advance from the ready position (Figure 8.1). As you advance, narrow the shooting angle, and shift into a semicrouch position (Figure 8.2).

the dribbler to cut the ball back toward the center of the goal, an action that widens the shooting angle. It is important that you dictate the movements of the attacker and not vice versa.

Shift into a crouch position (see Figure 8.3) as the opponent with the ball closes to within 10 yards. Extend your arms downward with palms forward and hands almost touching the ground beside your feet. The closer you get to the ball, the lower the crouch should be. In that position you will be less vulnerable to the low hard shot to either side.

Smothering the Ball

At the opportune moment you must go down to the ground on your side to smother the ball (see Figure 8.4). Positioning sideways provides greater coverage of the goal than does the headfirst or feetfirst dive. The headfirst dive has the added disadvantage of increasing the risk of serious injury.

Align your midsection with the ball when you are going to the ground. Your hands and arms cover the near-post area, while your feet and legs cover the far post. In that position you will be able to scramble on your hands to cover the ball if the opponent changes direction at the last moment and attempts to beat you by dribbling wide (toward the flank). If the opponent tries to cut the ball back toward the center of the goal, you can block the ball with your legs and feet.

Figures 8.3, 8.4   Assume the crouch position as you prepare to smother the ball (Figure 8.3). Then go to your side, providing a long barrier blocking the goal. Pin the ball to the ground with your hands (Figure 8.4).

When possible, extend your arms and hands to grab the ball rather than block it with your body. Both hands should be brought down with force, the bottom hand behind the ball to stop it and the upper hand on top of the ball to prevent a rebound. Once you have secured the ball, pull it in and cradle it against your chest. It is important that you remain on your side when you make the save. Rolling onto your stomach exposes your back and kidneys to an overly aggressive opponent and increases your chance of injury.

The most critical determinant for saving the breakaway is your ability to go to the ground at exactly the right moment. Read the dribbler's movements, anticipate when the shot will be taken, and dive to smother the ball (a) an instant before the shot is taken, (b) just as the shot is taken, or (c) an instant after the shot is taken. Diving too early, before the dribbler has committed, or too late, after the shot has been released, usually results in a goal against.

Saving a breakaway also requires a great deal of courage and determination. The play is not necessarily over, and the battle is not lost, if you fail to win the ball on your first attempt. Just the fact that you have forced the opponent to move into a poor shooting position may provide time for a second or even third attempt at covering the ball.

KEY ASPECTS OF PERFORMANCE

Smothering the Ball

- Advance with balance and control.
- Move forward quickly when the ball is not under the immediate control of the dribbler.
- Move forward more slowly when the ball is under the close control of the dribbler.
- Advance stride for stride with the dribbler as she or he approaches the penalty area.
- Begin your approach in an erect (ready) position, and crouch as you near the ball.
- Go to the ground sideways to obstruct the largest portion of the goal.
- Your arms and hands cover the near-post area of the goal; your feet and legs cover the center and far-post area.
- Anticipate the shot; don't go to the ground too early or too late.
- Extend your arms, and pin the ball with your hands to avoid a rebound.
- Remain on your side after making the save.

Drills

The following drills are designed to assist you in stopping the breakaway. All exercises should be clearly explained and demonstrated to you before you practice them. It is important that you do sufficient repetitions until you have mastered the movement. Most exercises are organized to simulate conditions that occur in and around the goal area and may be adapted to suit your own needs and abilities.

Breakaway Technique

B   A

Equipment: 2 balls

Organization: Two servers (A and B) face the goalkeeper at a distance of 5 yards. Server A is on the keeper's left, and B on the right; the keeper is in a crouch position.

Procedure: Server A dribbles toward the keeper, simulating a breakaway. The keeper goes to the ground and pins the ball. Immediately after the save the keeper returns to the crouch position. Server B repeats a breakaway from the opposite side. Continue for 30 seconds, rest, and repeat.

Breakdown Technique

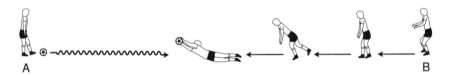

A   B

Equipment: 2 balls

Organization: Two goalkeepers (A and B) face one another at a distance of 20 yards.

Procedure: Goalkeeper A dribbles on a breakaway toward B, who begins his or her approach from the ready position. As the distance between the two closes, B crouches closer to the ground before finally going down on her or his side to save. Goalkeepers return to their original positions and repeat. Each attempts to save 10 breakaways.

Angles and Advancement

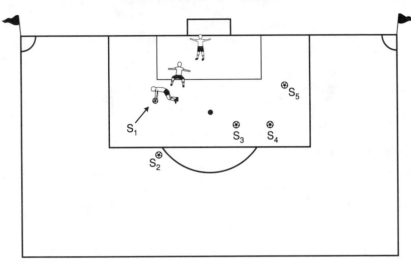

S = Servers

Equipment: 5 to 10 balls, 1 regulation-size goal

Organization: Several servers, each with a ball, position at various points in the penalty area. The goalkeeper positions to defend the goal.

Procedure: The keeper selects a server and moves toward him or her, gradually breaking down into a crouch position when nearing the ball. The server pushes the ball toward the goal and shoots just as the keeper goes to the ground to save. The server should not shoot until the keeper is close to the ground. After a save the keeper returns to the goal and then advances toward a different server.

Variation: Same setup, except that the server may elect to shoot or dribble past the keeper.

Leaving the Line

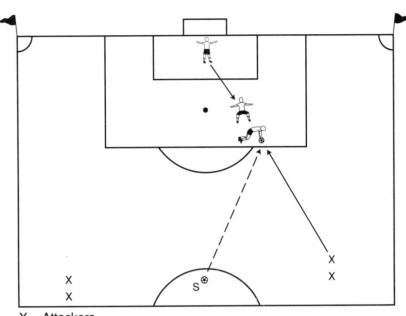

X = Attackers
S = Server

Equipment: 6 to 8 balls, 1 regulation-size goal

Organization: A server positions 35 yards from the goal, with a line of attackers positioned on each side.

Procedure: The server passes the ball to an attacker, who dribbles at top speed toward the goal on a breakaway. The goalkeeper advances stride for stride with the dribbler, shifts into a crouch when nearing the ball, and goes to the ground to save. Repeat several times.

Note: The server should vary the pace and distance of the pass, and the dribbler should vary the angle of approach to the goal.

Game-Simulated Breakaways

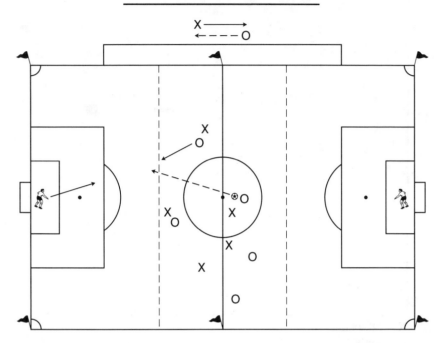

Equipment: 3 to 6 balls, 6 to 10 cones or markers, 1 regulation field, 2 regulation-size goals

Organization: Divide the field horizontally into three equal sections. Position a goal on each end of the field.

Procedure: Begin playing 5-on-5 in the middle sector. The team with possession of the ball attempts to score via the breakaway, either by dribbling into the attacking third or penetrating via the pass. Defending players are not allowed to enter their defending third of the field before the ball does. This restriction forces the goalkeeper to control that entire sector of the field and exposes the goalkeeper to a variety of breakaway situations. After each save the keeper should distribute the ball to a team-mate, who initiates an attack on the opposite goal.

CHAPTER **9**

Initiating the Attack: Goalkeeper Distribution

The goalkeeper is often viewed as a defensive specialist providing the all-important last line of defense. In a sense that is true, but the keeper also plays an important role in initiating the team's offensive attack. Accurate distribution of the ball is needed to ensure a smooth and quick transition from defense to attack. The most common methods of distribution are rolling, throwing, or kicking the ball. Become familiar with each technique; you will be required to use them all.

When deciding on which method of distribution to use, take into consideration several important guidelines:

- *Choose accuracy over distance.* When possible, the outlet pass should be played accurately to the feet of a teammate, where the ball can be easily controlled.
- *Vary the type of service.* Avoid letting your serves be predictable, so opponents cannot anticipate where and to whom you will roll, throw, or kick the ball.
- *Vary the direction of service.* As a general rule, distribute the ball into areas of the field where there are fewest opponents. The side of

the field opposite the position of the ball is often clear for an outlet pass.

- *Support the outlet pass.* Move forward out of the goal area after distributing the ball to a nearby teammate to make yourself available for a backpass.

Rolling

Use the rolling, or bowling, technique to distribute the ball over distances of 20 yards or less. Cup the ball in the palm of your hand, step toward the intended target, bend forward from your waist, and release the ball with a bowling-type motion. Release the ball at ground level in order to prevent bouncing (see Figures 9.1 and 9.2).

Figures 9.1, 9.2   When you distribute the ball by rolling, cup the ball in the palm of your hand and step toward the target (Figure 9.1). Release the ball at ground level to prevent it from bouncing (Figure 9.2).

Rolling the ball is most appropriate for dry, relatively flat surfaces. Use caution when field conditions are poor, because the ball may not roll true to form. The primary advantages of rolling the ball are quick release, accuracy, and ease of control. The major disadvantage is that this method of distribution can be used only over short distances.

Throwing

You can distribute the ball over medium and long distances by throwing or kicking. Throwing has two potential advantages over kicking—greater accuracy and quicker delivery. Three throwing techniques are used, depending on the distance and nature of the toss.

Sidearm Throw

The sidearm throw is generally used to distribute the ball over short and medium distances. In preparation to throw, draw your arm back and position it sideways at about shoulder height. Hold the ball in the palm of your hand (see Figure 9.3). Step toward the target as your throwing arm swings forward on a slightly downward plane. Release the ball at about waist height (see Figure 9.4). Snap your wrist downward upon release to generate a spinning motion on the ball, which will cause the ball to skim along the ground toward your target.

Figures 9.3, 9.4 Begin the sidearm throw by holding the ball in your palm at about shoulder height (Figure 9.3). While stepping toward the target, release the ball at about waist height, snapping your wrist downward upon release (Figure 9.4).

Baseball Throw

The baseball throw can be used to distribute the ball over distances of 25 to 35 yards. Release the ball with a motion similar to that used when tossing a baseball. Hold the ball in the palm of your throwing hand beside your head with your elbow flexed at 90 degrees (see Figure 9.5). Use a three-quarters or overhand throwing motion. To add velocity to the throw, snap your wrist forward toward the target upon release.

Primary advantages of the baseball throw are its quick release and direct line of trajectory to the target. You can also use the baseball throw

Figure 9.5 Begin the baseball throw with the ball held beside your head, with your elbow flexed about 90 degrees. Step toward the target and release the ball with an overhand throwing motion.

to toss the ball over the head of an opponent standing between you and the intended target.

Javelin Throw

The javelin throw is the most effective means of tossing the ball over long distances and, with minor alterations in the throwing motion, can also be used for shorter distances. Encase the ball in your fingers, palm, and wrist, with your arm fully extended behind your body. Hold the ball at approximately waist level (see Figure 9.6). The throwing motion moves along an upward arc, ending with a whiplike motion of the arm above the head. You can release the ball at any point along the throwing arc, depending upon the type of trajectory you desire. The sooner the ball is released, the higher the trajectory. Releasing the ball near the completion of your throwing motion will result in a flight trajectory almost parallel to the ground.

Arch your upper body backward from the vertical, and then snap forward at your waist to generate maximum distance on the throw. Step toward the target and use a complete follow-through motion of your throwing arm. Proper motion of the nonthrowing arm will generate added momentum to the throw. Point the nonthrowing arm diagonally upward in the direction of the target as you arch backward in preparation to deliver the ball. This arm should travel forward and then downward as the ball is released.

Figure 9.6   To use the javelin throw, encase the ball between your palm and wrist. Arch your upper body backward, with your throwing arm fully extended and the ball held at about waist level. Use a whiplike motion of your throwing arm along an upward arc to complete the throwing motion.

Kicking

Kicking is an effective means of distributing the ball over great distances. The principal advantage of kicking over throwing is that the ball can be quickly played into the opponent's half of the field. Its major limitation is that it isn't very accurate.

Depending upon the situation, you may use three kicking techniques. The punt and dropkick are used to distribute the ball after making a save or after receiving a backpass from a teammate. A goal kick is used to return a ball into play that traveled over the end line and was last touched by an opponent.

Full Volley Punt

Stand erect and face the target with your arms extended in front of your body. Hold the ball in the palm of the hand opposite your kicking foot (see Figure 9.7). Keep your head steady, and focus your vision on the ball. Step forward with the nonkicking foot, release the ball, and then volley the ball out of the air using a complete follow-through motion of the kicking leg. Extend and hold your kicking foot firm as the instep contacts the ball.

Figure 9.7   When executing the full volley punt, hold the ball in the hand opposite your kicking leg. This allows for greater follow-through motion of your kicking leg. Keep your head steady, with your upper body arched slightly forward and your vision focused on the ball.

Figure 9.8   To execute the dropkick, drop the ball from about waist height. Your kicking foot should meet the ball just as the ball contacts the ground. The instep of your kicking foot should be extended and firmly positioned, with your head steady and your vision focused on the ball.

Dropkick

The dropkick, or half volley, has the distinct advantage of combining distance with speed of delivery and can be used as an alternative to the full volley punt. Kicking mechanics are similar to those for the full volley punt, but, rather than the ball being volleyed directly out of the air, foot contact occurs just as the ball hits the ground. Position your nonkicking foot slightly behind and to the side of the ball at the moment of foot contact (see Figure 9.8).

Due to the velocity and low flight trajectory of the ball, a dropkick can be particularly effective on windy days. It is not advisable to use the dropkick when the field surface is wet or bumpy; if you slip or get an unexpected bounce, you might miskick in the goal area.

Table 9.1 outlines the advantages and disadvantages of, and tells when to use, the distribution methods we have discussed.

Goal Kick

The goal kick is used to return into play a ball that has traveled over the end line and was last touched by an opposing player. The kick must be taken from within the goal box, and the ball must leave the penalty area before touching another player. Oftentimes coaches designate a field player, usually one of the defenders, to take goal kicks. It is to the team's advantage, however, that the goalkeeper take goal kicks. This leaves the field player free to move forward into the midfield to support the attack. It is important, therefore, that you develop the ability and confidence to take goal kicks.

Use the lofted instep drive technique when taking a goal kick. Approach the ball from a slight angle, and plant your balance foot behind and slightly to the side of the ball. Square your shoulders with the intended target. Drive the instep of your kicking foot through the lower half of the ball with a powerful snaplike motion of the kicking leg. A complete follow-through motion is required to generate maximum distance on the kick.

Table 9.1   Goalkeeper's Distribution Chart

Type of service	Distance	Advantages	Disadvantages
Rolling (bowling)	20 yards or less	Quick release, accuracy, easiest method for receiver to control as ball stays on the ground	Can only be used for limited distances and when defenders are playing off the receiver
Sidearm throw	15-30 yards	Ball stays low for easier control, quick release, more velocity than rolling ball	Can only be used for limited distances; poor release will cause ball to take a high bounce
Baseball throw	20-35 yards	Quick release, direct line of trajectory, can throw over an opponent	Difficult ball to receive unless right on a teammate's foot; improper release can result in abnormal spinning and inaccurate throws
Javelin throw	30 yards or more	Most common method; throwing motion can be altered to achieve a variety of distances, including beyond midfield; can be thrown with great accuracy	Slower release makes it easier for defenders to read and intercept; a higher trajectory may make control more difficult for the receiver
Full volley punt	45 yards or more	Distance, quick way into attack half of the field, can eliminate a team of defenders with one kick	Highly inaccurate, chances much greater of losing possession than any other method, high trajectory makes it very easy to read and intercept
Dropkick (1/2 volley)	40 yards or more	Distance, lower trajectory allows for greater velocity. A well-struck half volley can also eliminate several opposing players and can be delivered faster and more accurately than a full volley punt	Risky method on a wet day or on a poor field, very difficult ball to receive, miskicks are common and could result in a dangerous counter-attack

---

KEY ASPECTS OF PERFORMANCE

Distributing the Ball

- Distribute the ball with the primary objective of maintaining possession.
- Use the rolling (bowling) technique to distribute the ball over short distances.
- Use the sidearm throw or baseball throw over medium distances.
- Use the javelin throw, the full volley punt, or the dropkick to distribute the ball over long distances.
- Develop the ability to take goal kicks.
- Be prepared to move beyond the penalty area to play balls with your feet.

Drills

The following drills are designed to improve your throwing and kicking skills. All exercises should be clearly explained and demonstrated to you before you practice them. It is important that you do sufficient repetitions until you have mastered the movement. Most exercises are organized to simulate conditions that occur in and around the goal area and may be adapted to suit your own needs and abilities.

Throwing

Target Throwing

Equipment: 2 balls, tape, a wall or kickboard

Organization: Use tape to mark a 3-foot-by-3-foot target area on a wall or kickboard.

Procedure: Practice throwing a ball at the target from various angles and distances. Award yourself 1 point for each time you hit the target.

Distribution Technique

Equipment: 1 ball

Organization: Goalkeepers pair up and practice distributing the ball to one another over various distances. Execute 10 repetitions of each of the following types of distribution.

- Rolling balls—10 to 20 yards
- Sidearm throw—15 to 25 yards
- Baseball throw—20 to 35 yards
- Javelin throw—35 yards and above

Variation: Same setup, except that keepers distribute the ball to a moving target.

Distribution Circuit

Equipment: 1 ball, regulation field

Organization: Four goalkeepers (A, B, C, D) position at various locations throughout the playing field: Keeper A positions in a goal. Keeper B positions outside of the penalty area near the touchline. Keeper C positions in the center circle. Keeper D positions within the opposite penalty area.

Procedure: Goalkeeper A distributes the ball by rolling, or using the sidearm throw to Keeper B, who receives the ball and uses the baseball throw to toss it to Keeper C. Keeper C receives the ball and uses the javelin throw to toss it to Keeper D. Keeper D punts or dropkicks the ball back to Keeper A. Repeat the circuit 5 times, then rotate positions and repeat 5 more times. Continue to rotate positions until each keeper has practiced all three methods of distribution.

Variation: Same setup, except that each goalkeeper plays the ball into the space ahead of the receiving player. The goalkeeper then follows his or her pass to the next position in the circuit. Emphasize accuracy and correct pace.

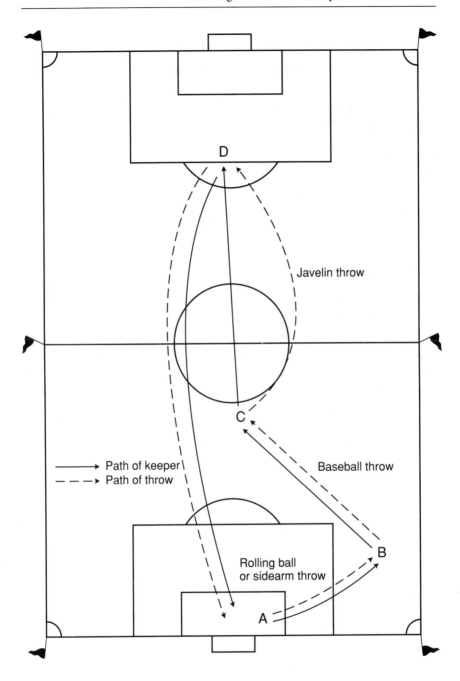

D

Javelin throw

C

Baseball throw

Path of keeper
Path of throw

Rolling ball
or sidearm throw

B

A

Kicking

Kicking Technique

Equipment: 2 balls, kickboard or regulation-size goal

Organization: Two goalkeepers face each other 10 yards apart.

Procedure: Partners volley or half-volley a ball back and forth at each other's chest.

Variation: Goalkeepers practice volleys, half volleys, or goal kicks off of a wall or kickboard or into the net of a regulation-size goal.

Target Kicking

Equipment: 6 to 12 balls, 12 to 24 cones or markers

Organization: Mark off several 10-yard-by-10-yard grids at various sections of the playing field. Position grids at different distances from the goal.

Procedure: Two goalkeepers compete against one another using punts, dropkicks, and goal kicks in an attempt to distribute the ball into the grids. Each goalkeeper is awarded 2 points for each ball that enters a grid on the fly and 1 point for a ball that rolls into a grid. Keepers alternate turns kicking the ball. The first player to total 20 points wins the competition.

Variation: Reduce or enlarge the size of grids.

CHAPTER 10

Defending Restart Situations

Restarts, or set plays, include corner kicks, throw-ins, direct and indirect free kicks, and penalty kicks. Restart situations provide excellent scoring opportunities, because they are one of the few times during a soccer match that a team can execute a planned play. Defending against restart situations provides one of your greatest challenges.

The Corner Kick

Position in the center or front third of the goal (nearest the ball) about 1 to 3 yards off of the goal line. Assume an open stance facing forward so you can view as much of the penalty area as possible (see Figure 10.1). From this position you can keep the ball in sight and you're also aware of opponents stationed in the area front and center of the goal. Do not face the corner of the field with shoulders square to where the ball is spotted! In that position your vision of the penalty area is limited, and you will also have difficulty handling a ball crossed to the far-post area of the goal. Your exact position in the goal will vary depending on your

Figure 10.1   Use an open stance with your shoulders square to the playing field when you defend a corner kick. Focus your vision on the ball, but remain aware of opponents positioned front and center of the goal.

ability to handle crossed balls, the type of corner-kick plays run by the opponents, the heading abilities of opponents and your teammates, and the width of the field.

Although the tactics used to defend against corner kicks may vary from one team to another, there are four critical areas where defending players should position to help their goalkeeper. One player fronts the ball at a distance of 10 yards to prevent the ball from being driven to the near post. This individual is also in position to apply pressure should the attacking team try a "short corner," where the kicker passes the ball to a nearby teammate, who then crosses the ball. A second player positions inside the near post facing upfield. This player is responsible for stopping any shot to the near-post corner of the goal that beats the keeper. A third player positions on the 6-yard line, just about even with the near post, and is responsible for clearing a ball driven into that area. A fourth player positions to cover the far-post area of the goalmouth (see Figure 10.2). All remaining players either mark an opponent or position in zone coverage, depending upon the coach's philosophy. All defenders should be goalside and ballside of an opponent at the moment the kick is taken.

The Throw-In

A throw-in is used primarily to return the ball into play after it has crossed over a touchline. In recent years, however, the long throw-in has evolved

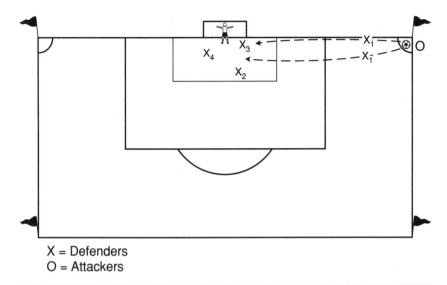

X = Defenders
O = Attackers

Figure 10.2 When you defend a corner kick, position your teammates to protect four critical areas of the goalmouth. Player X_1 positions along the end line, 10 yards from the ball, to prevent a low kick from being driven into the near-post area of the goal. Player X_2 positions on the 6-yard line about even with the near post. Player X_3 stands next to the near post to prevent the ball from being driven through that area and across the goalmouth. Player X_4 positions to protect the far-post area of the goal. All other defenders should mark opponents in the goal area.

into a dangerous scoring weapon as well. Many players have developed the ability to throw the ball 30 yards or farther. As a consequence, whenever a throw-in is taken from within the defending third of the field, you must be prepared for the possibility of the ball being tossed directly into the goalmouth. Most teams defend against the long throw-in the same way they defend against a corner kick.

Direct and Indirect Free Kicks

Free kicks taken from within shooting range of the goal provide excellent scoring opportunities for the attacking team. Although the goalkeeper plays a significant role, successfully defending against free kicks requires the organization and involvement of all team members.

When the opposing team is awarded a free kick, immediately position yourself to have a clear view of the ball in the event of a quick kick. At the same time, several of your teammates should position side by side to form a wall 10 yards from the ball. The number of players in the wall depends upon the location of the ball and the ability of the kicker. For example, a free kick spotted front and center of the goal requires more players in the wall than does a ball spotted on the flank, where the shooting angle to goal is narrower (see Figure 10.3). It is your responsibility to verbally and visually communicate to teammates how many players you want in the wall. Players not involved in the wall mark opponents in the vicinity of the goal.

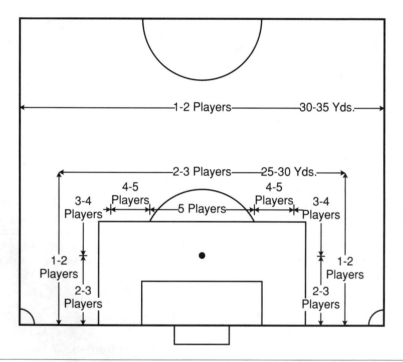

Figure 10.3 General guidelines exist for determining how many defenders should position when forming a wall. The number of players in the wall depends upon the position of the ball and the ability of the opposing player taking the kick.

Setting a wall requires a great deal of planning and organization. One player is generally designated to "post" the wall. The post player has the responsibility of anchoring the wall by quickly moving to a position directly between the ball and near post (see Figure 10.4). Most teams designate a field player, preferably one of the forwards, to help align the post player with the near post. Other players in the wall line up to the inside of the post player. The wall is positioned to block a shot to the near-post area; the goalkeeper positions to protect the other half of the goal.

Of particular concern are indirect free kicks taken from within the penalty area. In this situation anywhere from 6 to 10 people may be used in the wall, depending upon the distance and angle of the ball from the

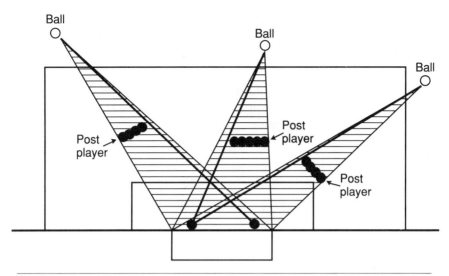

Figure 10.4 When teammates form a wall, the post player positions between the ball and the near post of the goal. Teammates line up to the inside of the post player.

goal. The keeper generally positions behind the wall in line with the ball except in situations where the ball is within 10 yards of the goal and the wall is positioned on the goal line. In that instance you should position in front of the wall and in direct line with the ball.

The Penalty Kick

A penalty kick is a direct free kick taken from a spot 12 yards front and center of the goal. It is purely a one-on-one situation—the keeper versus the shooter. No other players are allowed within the penalty area or penalty arc until the shot has been taken. Saving a penalty kick may be your most difficult challenge—although the pressure is actually on the kicker, because in most instances the keeper is not expected to make the save.

Federation International de Football Association (FIFA) Law #14 states that the goalkeeper must stand on the goal line without moving his or her feet until the ball has been played. You are permitted to move your upper body back and forth to distract the kicker, but wild antics (shouting, waving your arms, etc.) are considered poor sportsmanship and are prohibited. The referee will allow you to set in position before the whistle that signals the kicker to initiate the penalty shot.

In preparation to defend a penalty kick, assume a posture similar to the basic ready position. Lean slightly forward, with your weight evenly distributed and centered over the balls of your feet. To save, vault sideways parallel to the goal line or even slightly forward to reduce the shooting angle. If you cannot hold the ball, box or deflect it wide of the goal.

To improve your chances of saving a penalty shot, look for subtle hints that might suggest where the ball will be directed. Pay particular attention to the kicker just before and during her or his approach to the ball. Look for the following cues (based upon a right-footed kicker), which may tip you off to the kicker's intentions.

Before the Kick

- Watch the opponent's eyes. He or she may unconsciously stare toward the area of the goal where the ball will be directed.

During Approach to Ball

- If the kicker approaches the ball at a sharp angle (greater than 60 degrees), most likely she or he will kick the ball to your left. From an angled approach it is difficult for the shooter to pull the ball back to the right corner of the goal.
- If the kicker approaches from directly behind the ball, it is likely that he or she will aim the ball to your right.
- If the kicking foot is turned sideways, the shooter will have to push the ball to your left with the inside of the foot.
- If the kicking foot is positioned down and inward, the kicker will probably use the instep drive to shoot the ball to your right.
- Watch the kicker's hips as she or he approaches the ball. The hips will usually square with the intended target (area of the goal) just prior to the kick.

Note

You can improve your technique for saving penalty kicks through repeated practice in matchlike situations. Set aside adequate time to practice this important aspect of goalkeeping.

CHAPTER 11

Fitness: The Cornerstone of Optimal Performance

It is a common misconception that a goalkeeper need not be physically fit. Though you may not need the same level of aerobic conditioning as a field player who runs several miles during a game, you do need an adequate level of overall body fitness to effectively meet the demands of the position. Although fitness alone does not guarantee that you will become an outstanding goalkeeper, without a sufficient level of fitness you certainly will not achieve your full potential.

The primary components of goalkeeper fitness include flexibility and agility, muscle strength, and muscle endurance. Flexibility and agility involve your range of motion, which is essential for properly executing goalkeeper skills. You need muscle strength to vault your body across the goal when making a save or jumping up among a crowd of players to receive a high crossed ball. Muscle endurance is the ability to sustain effort for a prolonged period of time. Without endurance your muscles tire sooner, which diminishes skill performance and increases mental errors. The unfit goalkeeper is also more susceptible to injury, which further diminishes performance capability.

This chapter provides an overview of the essential components of goal-keeper fitness. You can also incorporate into your training program many of the drills and exercises discussed in previous chapters.

Warm-Up and Cool-Down

Before you participate in strenuous exercise, do a warm-up that physically and mentally prepares you for more vigorous activity. Warm-up exercises serve several useful functions. Muscle temperatures are elevated, which promotes increased blood flow. This in turn results in improved muscle contraction and reflex time, increases suppleness, helps prevent muscle soreness, and helps prevent muscle and joint injuries. The duration of your warm-up may vary depending upon your individual needs and the environmental conditions (temperature, humidity, etc.), but as a general rule you should warm up for 15 to 25 minutes. Warm-up activities should be intense enough to cause sweating, an indication that your muscle temperatures have increased.

Any activity that involves the large muscle groups can be considered a warm-up. A *related warm-up* consists of movements that are commonly used during performance of your sport. For the goalkeeper this would include various types of foot movements (side shuffle, power step, etc.) and ball-handling exercises (ball gymnastics) as well as flexibility and agility exercises. An *unrelated warm-up* does not use sport-specific move-ments. Jumping jacks, sit-ups, toe raises, push-ups, and half-squats are examples of activities for an unrelated warm-up. Both related and un-related warm-ups can create the desired physiological changes, but when you can, use a related warm-up, because a practice effect may also be realized.

At the end of each practice or game, take a few minutes to allow your body to "cool down." Select a stretching exercise for each major muscle group and thoroughly stretch that area. Be sure to include the hamstrings, quadriceps, groin, and back. Stretching during the cool-down period will help prevent next-day soreness.

Note

Do not bounce or jerk when stretching your muscles. Such movement, often called "ballistic stretching," may cause minor tissue damage to your muscles. It is best to perform static stretches, in which you slowly assume the stretch position, hold that position for a period of 15 to 30 seconds, relax, and then repeat the stretch (see the next section, "Flexibility").

Sample Warm-Up

5 minutes: Light jogging while

1. bouncing a ball and catching it at waist height with your hands in W position; and
2. tossing a ball above your head and catching it at the highest possible point; and
3. rolling a ball 5 or 6 yards in front, moving to it, and scooping it to your chest; and
4. side shuffling while bouncing a ball and receiving it with your hands in W position.

10 minutes: Flexibility exercises (static stretching done with a ball)

10 minutes: Perform the following ball-handling exercises for 2 minutes each:

1. The goalkeeper sits in a V position facing a server 2 yards away. The server tosses the ball to the side of the keeper, who catches and returns it. The server quickly tosses to the other side, and the keeper catches it. Continue tosses in rapid succession.
2. The goalkeeper stands facing a server 5 yards away. The keeper rolls a ball to the server, who kicks it back at the keeper. The keeper receives the ball with proper technique. Repeat in rapid succession.
3. Two goalkeepers face each other at a distance of 8 yards while rapidly volleying a ball back and forth.
4. Two keepers face each other at a distance of 10 yards. One rolls a ball to the side of the other, who uses a collapse step to fall to the ground and pin the ball. After saving, the keeper jumps to his or her feet and rolls a ball that the other must save. Repeat in rapid succession.
5. The goalkeeper positions in a regulation-size goal, shuffling along an arc from one goal post to the other. A server positions 8 to 12 yards front and center of the goal with a supply of balls and kicks or volleys balls at the keeper, who saves while shuffling along the arc.

Flexibility

Flexibility is the range of possible movement around a joint or series of joints. Poor flexibility can limit athletic performance, particularly for the goalkeeper. Static stretching is the preferred method of increasing your range of motion: Slowly extend the target muscle or group of muscles to the greatest possible length without discomfort. A slow extension is preferred, because this will inhibit firing of the stretch reflex. Hold the stretch position for 15 to 30 seconds, then relax, and then gently move into a deeper stretch for 15 to 30 seconds. To prevent muscle injury, do not bounce or jerk when stretching.

Individuals may vary greatly in flexibility, because movement around any particular joint depends on a number of factors. For example, flexibility of the hip joint is limited by tendons and ligaments, muscle development, and joint capsules. Movement of other joints, such as the elbow and knee, is limited by bone and skeletal structure. As a consequence, flexibility exercises should never become an arena of competition among teammates. Measure your progress against your own standards and your initial state of flexibility. The ultimate objective is to improve your range of motion in a safe, injury-free manner. Understand your capabilities, and stretch accordingly.

Flexibility exercises should be used daily in the off-season and before practice or game competition in season. Use the following exercises to improve your flexibility.

Exercises

Static Stretch Exercises

Sitting Hamstring Stretch

Begin in a sitting position with both legs straight. Bend your right knee and slide your heel toward your buttocks, keeping the outer side of your right calf and thigh on the ground. Place your right heel against the inside of your left thigh. Keep your left leg straight as you bend forward at the waist. Hold the stretch position for 15 to 30 seconds, relax, and then repeat.

Bent-Leg Hamstring Stretch

Lie on your back with knees bent and feet flat on the ground. Place your right hand behind your left ankle and your left hand behind your left thigh. Flex at the hip, and pull gently on your calf until you feel the stretch. Hold for 15 or 30 seconds, relax, and then repeat. Repeat using your right leg.

Lying on Side Quad Stretch

Lie on your left side, using your left forearm for support. Flex your right leg and grab your right ankle with your right hand. Slowly pull the leg back until you feel a good stretch in your upper thigh. Be careful not to hyperextend your back while pulling your leg. Hold the stretch position for 15 to 30 seconds, rest, and then repeat with the other leg. Perform 2 repetitions for each leg.

Lying on Stomach Quad Stretch

Lie on your stomach with legs straight. Flex one leg and bring the heel toward your buttock. Reach back with your arm, grasp your ankle, and slowly pull your heel toward your buttocks until you feel a stretch. Hold that position for 15 to 30 seconds. Rest and then repeat the stretch with the other leg. Perform 2 repetitions with each leg.

Push-Up Stretch for Calf

Assume a push-up position. Place one foot on top of the heel of the other foot. Slowly push backward with your arms, and try to touch the heel of your balance foot to the ground. Push as far as possible without pain, and hold that position for 15 to 30 seconds. Repeat 2 times with each leg.

Sitting Groin Stretch

Assume a sitting position with the soles of your feet touching in front of you. Place your elbows on the inside surface of your legs just above the knees. Gently push down on the inside of your knees. Hold the stretch for 15 to 30 seconds, relax, and then repeat.

Lying Groin Stretch

Lie flat on your back. Flex your knees, and place the heels and soles of your feet together in front of you. Spread your legs as far as you can as you try to lower the outside area of each knee as close to the ground as possible. Hold the stretch for 15 to 30 seconds, relax, and then repeat.

Standing Lower Back Stretch

Stand with your feet spread, knees slightly flexed, and a ball on the ground beneath you. Bend forward at the waist, cross your arms, and try to touch one elbow to the ball. Hold the stretch for 15 to 30 seconds, relax, and then repeat with the opposite elbow. Perform 2 repetitions for each elbow.

Head Turns

Turn your head as far as possible toward the left. Hold that position for 15 to 30 seconds, then turn your head to the right. Perform 2 repetitions in each direction.

Static Neck Stretch

Place your right hand on the left side of your head. Use your hand to slowly pull your head down and sideways toward your right shoulder. Do not jerk! Hold that position for 15 to 30 seconds and relax. Repeat the stretch to the opposite side.

Ball Gymnastic Exercises

Sitting Lower Back Stretch

Equipment: A soccer ball

Procedure: Assume a sitting position with legs together and knees flexed. Slowly roll a soccer ball in a complete circle around your feet and your back. Try to keep both hands on the ball at all times. Repeat 10 times in one direction, then reverse direction for 10 repetitions.

Figure Eights

Equipment: A soccer ball

Procedure: Assume the same position as for the standing lower back stretch. Roll the ball in a figure eight around and through your legs. Repeat 10 times in one direction. Reverse direction for 10 repetitions.

Windmills

Equipment: A soccer ball

Procedure: Stand holding a ball, with your legs spread shoulder-width apart. Bend forward at the waist and perform large circles in front of your body with the ball. Repeat 5 times in one direction, then reverse direction for 5 circles. Perform the circles in a slow and controlled manner.

Partner Trunk Rotations

Equipment: A soccer ball

Procedure: Stand back to back with a partner, about 1 yard apart. Exchange a ball with your partner by twisting at the waist and exchanging the ball behind you, then turn and exchange in the opposite direction. Repeat for 30 ball exchanges.

Quick Turns

Equipment: A soccer ball

Procedure: Hold a ball between your legs, with one hand behind and one hand in front of your legs. Change hands from back to front, and catch the ball before it drops to the ground. Repeat at maximum speed for 30 seconds.

Cushion and Catch

Equipment: 2 soccer balls

Procedure: Partners face each other at a distance of 3 yards. Each holds a soccer ball in her or his left hand at about head height. On command, partners simultaneously toss from their left hand to their partner's right hand. Players must receive the ball, and return the toss, with one hand. Continue for 50 tosses.

Bounce and Catch

Equipment: A soccer ball

Procedure: While slowly jogging forward, bounce a ball hard off the ground. Catch the rebound using both hands in the *W* position before the ball reaches waist height.

Muscle Strength and Endurance

The ability to sustain activity over an extended period of time is commonly referred to as *endurance capacity*. Most sports require two types of endurance; (a) general, or cardiovascular, endurance (aerobic fitness), and (b) local, or muscle, endurance (anaerobic fitness). *General endurance* is the ability of the circulatory system to provide sufficient oxygen to the working muscles. It involves gross body movements, with a large percentage of the body's muscle groups working simultaneously. *Muscle endurance* is more specific and involves localized use of a small percentage of the body's musculature.

Although the goalkeeper should develop an adequate level of cardiovascular fitness for overall health and well-being, local muscle endurance is more specific to game performance. For example, the specific muscles located in the upper thighs and quadriceps are used extensively during the match for jumping, punting, diving, and quick changes of direction when reacting to a shot. The muscles of your chest and arms come into use when you dive with your arms extended to save a shot, or when you scramble on your hands and arms to cover a loose ball. In games where you are very active, muscle fatigue due to a lack of muscular endurance may limit your ability to come up with the big play when it's needed. It is essential, therefore, that you develop a high level of muscle endurance in the muscles of your thighs as well as in your shoulders, arms, and chest.

Muscle strength is the ability to overcome a force or resistance. In sports that involve speed, power, and explosive movement, strength gains generally translate into improved performance. This is particularly important for the goalkeeper, who must possess the power and explosiveness needed to vault through the air with her or his body fully extended to save powerful shots. Weight, or resistance, training is the most common method used to increase strength and develop muscle mass. Weight training is also one of the most misunderstood concepts in athletics. The fear of becoming muscle-bound and inflexible has discouraged many athletes from participating in strength-training programs. In truth, a properly supervised weight-training program promotes the development of muscle strength and endurance while improving an athlete's overall flexibility.

A controversial issue among coaches, educators, trainers, physicians, and parents involves the age at which young athletes should begin training with weights. There are three primary concerns: (a) Improper technique can result in damage to the growth center of a developing bone, (b) there is the potential for injury to connective tissue, and (c) prior to puberty, young athletes lack sufficient levels of certain hormones needed to stimulate the muscle development that normally results from weight training. Research suggests that these are valid concerns. As a rule of thumb, preadolescent children should use caution when participating in a strength program. Rather than using free weights (dumbbells, etc.) for resistance, young athletes (and old alike) can use their own body weight as the resistance to be moved. For example, a variety of push-ups, pull-ups, dips, and abdominal exercises can provide young athletes the same basic strength-training benefits as "weight training" without endangering their development. Such exercises are equally beneficial for mature athletes.

Muscle Strength and Endurance Exercises

The following exercises use your own body weight as the resistance to be moved and can be used to develop both muscle strength and endurance. If you wish to undertake an actual weight-training program, consult with an expert who can devise a regimen best suited to your needs and expectations.

Abdominal Exercises

Curls

Lie flat on the ground with your knees flexed and your arms folded across your chest. Rise up slowly until your upper back is raised approximately 45 degrees off the floor. Your lower back should remain on or near the ground. Lower yourself slowly to the ground and repeat. Do not perform this exercise with your hands behind your neck or head, because you do not want to pull on your head. Perform 15 to 30 repetitions.

Wall Sit-Ups

Sit with your legs positioned up against the waist of a standing partner. Keep your legs straight as you sit up and touch your hands to your toes. Repeat 15 to 30 times.

Sit-Up and Ball Exchange

Partners sit facing one another with interlocked ankles and perform sit-ups, exchanging a ball between them each time they sit up. Repeat 30 to 40 sit-ups in a slow and controlled manner.

Leg Exercises

Knees to Chest

From a standing position, jump and bring your knees up to your chest. Repeat at maximum speed for 30 seconds, rest, and repeat again.

Walk-Ups

Stand facing a bench about 12 to 15 inches high. Step up onto the bench with one foot and then the other. Immediately step down with one foot, then the other, and then repeat the exercise. Use a four-count rhythm (e.g., up, up, down, down). Perform 20 to 30 repetitions, rest, then repeat.

Over and Back

Stand beside a stationary ball. Keep your feet together as you jump back and forth over the ball. Take care not to step on the ball. If you have difficulty jumping over the ball, stand slightly behind or in front of it as you jump. Repeat at maximum speed for 30 seconds, rest, and repeat.

Upper Body Exercises

Regular Push-Ups

Assume a push-up position, supporting your body weight with your arms and legs. Your hands should be approximately shoulder-width apart, with your legs straight behind you. Slowly lower your body until your chest touches the ground, then use your arms to rise to the starting position. Do not let your body sag. Do as many repetitions as you can.

Ball Push-Ups

Assume a push-up position with your hands on top of a soccer ball. Slowly lower your body until your chest touches the ball, then raise yourself to the starting position. Do not let your body sag. Do as many repetitions as you can.

Walking Push-Ups

Assume a push-up position with a ball in front of you. Support your body weight with your arms and legs. Walk forward on your hands as you nudge the ball with your forehead. Don't allow your knees to touch the ground or your body to sag. Walk forward for 20 yards, rest, and repeat.

Decline Push-Ups

Assume a push-up position with your ankles resting on the shoulders of a standing partner. Support your body weight with your arms. Slowly lower your body until your chest touches the ground, then raise yourself to the starting position. Repeat as many times as possible.

Wheelbarrow Walk

Assume a push-up position with a partner holding your legs. Walk forward on your hands for 20 yards. This is not a race; proceed in a slow and controlled manner.

Pull-Ups

Grab an overhead bar, with your hands approximately shoulder-width apart. Pull your body upward until your chin is level with the bar, then slowly lower yourself to the starting position. Repeat as many times as possible.

Plyometrics

Plyometric, or jump, training is an effective method for developing explosive power, an important physiological component of goalkeeper performance. Plyometric training originated in Europe and emphasizes the improvement of speed and strength, which translates into increased power. In its simplest terms, plyometric training enhances the ability of muscles or groups of muscles to respond more quickly and powerfully to changes in muscle length. Many goalkeeping skills, such as jumping up to receive a high ball or vaulting sideways to save a shot, involve lengthening (eccentric) muscle contractions rapidly followed by shortening (concentric) contractions. The more quickly the concentric contraction follows the eccentric contraction, the greater the power generated. Plyometric exercises are designed to shorten, or speed up, the eccentric-concentric contraction phase.

Plyometric training is a particularly effective method of developing explosive leg power in the goalkeeper. Most exercises are easy to learn and involve rapid changes of direction such as skipping, bounding, hopping, or jumping.

For more information on plyometric training, see *Plyometrics: Explosive Power Training* by James Radcliffe and Robert Farentinos, Human Kinetics Publishers, 1985; or *Jumping Into Plyometrics* by Don Chu, Human Kinetics Publishers, 1991.

Plyometric Exercises

Double-Leg Hop

Stand upright with your back straight, shoulders facing forward, and arms at your sides. Begin by jumping up and flexing your legs to bring your feet under your buttocks. Upon landing, immediately jump up again. Try to jump as high as possible. Repeat 15 to 20 jumps, rest, and repeat.

Single-Leg Hop

This exercise is similar to the double-leg hop, except that all of the jumping is done on one leg. The opposite leg is held in a flexed position while you jump. Perform 6 to 10 repetitions on one leg, then repeat with the opposite leg. Perform 2 sets with each leg.

Sideways Hop

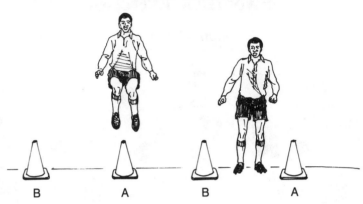

Position 2 cones side by side approximately 2 yards apart. Stand beside one of the cones with your feet together and toes straight ahead. Jump sideways over the first cone, then over the second. Immediately change direction and jump back over the second cone, then the first. Continue the back-and-forth sequence for 30 seconds. Rest for 1 minute, then repeat for 30 seconds.

Bench Jump

Stand about 2 feet from an 18- to 24-inch-high bench. Using your arms to generate upward momentum, jump up onto the bench and land with your feet together. Immediately jump back to the ground and repeat the jump. Continue at maximum speed for 10 to 12 repetitions, rest, and then repeat. (Refer to Figure 3.18 on page 22.)

High Knee Action Skipping

This exercise provides excellent practice of the technique used to jump when fielding a high crossed ball. Begin in a standing position with one leg slightly ahead of the other. Driving off of the back leg, thrust the opposite leg up as you jump as high as possible. Upon landing, immediately repeat the action with the opposite leg. Remember to thrust your arms up to generate added momentum. Perform 3 sets of 8 to 12 skips.

Year-Round Training Program

Fitness training is not merely a seasonal concern—it requires year-round effort. Plan your training regimen around three periods of time: the off-season, preseason, and in season.

Off-season conditioning should focus on improving muscle strength and endurance, flexibility, and agility. Also emphasize developing proper footwork and "soft hands" to catch and hold the ball. Recreational activities such as racquetball, tennis, handball, and squash will help improve your quickness and eye-hand coordination.

Preseason conditioning should include more game-related fitness drills. Include a ball whenever possible. The primary focus of preseason conditioning should be to sharpen skills, develop game-related fitness, and prepare you both mentally and physically for actual game competition.

In-season training should focus on maintaining a maximum state of readiness. Functional and pressure training drills should comprise the bulk of in-season drills. Less time should be devoted to pure fitness training, because it takes less work to maintain a high level of fitness than it does to develop a high level of fitness.

Laws and the Goalkeeper

The Federation International de Football Association (FIFA) is the governing body of soccer throughout the world. The official FIFA laws comprise 17 rules that govern play on the soccer field. Although a thorough understanding of all FIFA laws is essential, several rules apply more directly than others to the goalkeeper. The following material provides an overview of the FIFA laws that are of particular significance to the goalkeeper.

The Field of Play

The *soccer goal* is 8 yards wide and 8 feet tall. The goal is positioned on the midpoint of the goal line within the goal area. Protecting 192 square feet of goal space is no easy task, and the keeper must use every means available to cover the area.

The *goal area* is a rectangular box drawn along each goal line. It is formed by two lines drawn at right angles to the goal line, 6 yards from each goalpost. These lines extend 6 yards onto the field of play and are joined by a line drawn parallel to the goal line. The goalkeeper cannot be legally "charged" within the goal area. Goal kicks are also taken from within the goal area.

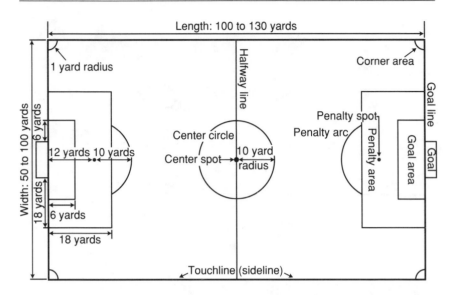

The *penalty area* is a rectangular box drawn along each endline. The penalty area is formed by two lines perpendicular to the goal line, 18 yards from each goalpost. These lines extend 18 yards onto the field and are connected by a line drawn parallel to the goal line. The goalkeeper is permitted use of the hands to control the ball within the penalty area. If the keeper leaves the penalty area to play the ball, he or she loses that privilege.

The *penalty spot* is located within the penalty area 12 yards front and center of the midpoint of the goal line. Penalty kicks are taken from the penalty spot. When a penalty kick is taken, all players, except the kicker and the goalkeeper must position outside of the penalty area and be at least 10 yards from the ball.

A *penalty arc* line, having a radius of 10 yards from the penalty spot, is drawn outside of the penalty area. This restraining arc delineates the area outside of the penalty area into which field players cannot enter until the penalty kick has been taken. Note that the area enclosed within the penalty arc is not considered part of the penalty area, so the goalkeeper is not permitted use of the hands to control the ball within the penalty arc. The penalty for illegal use of the hands is a direct kick awarded the opposing team from the spot of the infraction.

Equipment

The FIFA laws state that the color of her or his uniform must adequately distinguish the goalkeeper from field players and the officials. The referee has the authority to order the goalkeeper to change jersey colors in compliance with this rule. (For additional information on goalkeeper equipment, see chapter 1.)

Method of Scoring

A goal is scored when the ball passes completely over the goal line, between the uprights and under the crossbar, provided it has not been thrown, carried, or intentionally propelled by the arm or hand of a field player on the attacking team. The goalkeeper is the only player on the team who is permitted to intentionally propel the ball, by hand or arm, into the opposing goal, provided the keeper is within his or her own penalty area when attempting the throw. Few, if any, goalkeepers possess the physical ability to accomplish that feat.

Fouls and Misconduct

Fouls are punishable by the award of either a *direct* or *indirect* free kick. Recent rule changes by FIFA have increased the severity of penalties applied to these fouls. Specifically, any player, including the goalkeeper, who intentionally fouls an opponent who is moving toward the goal with an obvious opportunity to score shall be sent off for serious foul play. An example of this rule application would be the goalkeeper's deliberately holding, tripping, or pushing an opponent who is in an obvious position to score. A direct free kick shall be awarded to the opposing team from the place where the infraction occurred. Two important criteria must be met before a player is sent off. The opponent must be in an "obvious position" to score and the foul must be "intentional." If in her or his opinion these two criteria are not met, the referee may still signal a foul, but a send-off of the player committing the foul is not warranted.

A goalkeeper who commits one of the following offenses within his or her own penalty area is penalized by the award of a direct free kick (penalty kick) to the opposing team.

- Kicking an opponent
- Tripping an opponent
- Jumping at (leaving the ground with both feet when jumping to tackle) an opponent
- Charging an opponent in a violent or dangerous manner
- Charging an opponent from behind, unless the opponent is illegally obstructing the goalkeeper from the ball

- Striking an opponent
- Holding an opponent
- Pushing an opponent

A goalkeeper who commits one of the following offenses will be penalized by the award to the opposing team of an indirect free kick from the spot of the infraction.

- Playing in a manner that the referee considers to be dangerous to the goalkeeper or to other players
- Intentionally obstructing an opponent when not attempting to play the ball
- After gaining possession of the ball, releasing the ball and then controlling or picking up the ball again before it has left the penalty area or has been played by an opponent (this foul is generally referred to as "double possession")
- Taking more than four steps while in possession of the ball without releasing it

Three fouls are of particular significance to the goalkeeper: (a) charging against the goalkeeper by an opposing player, (b) double possession, and (c) the four-step possession rule.

Charging

It is legal for a field player to charge the goalkeeper when playing the ball if one or both feet remain on the ground and contact is limited to shoulder to shoulder. The field player is not permitted to extend her or his arms outward from the body.

The goalkeeper can be legally charged at the following times:

- When in possession of the ball
- When obstructing an opponent
- When positioned outside of the goal area

It is *illegal* to charge the goalkeeper within the goal area if he or she is not in possession of the ball. Violation of this rule results in an indirect free kick awarded to the goalkeeper's team at the spot of the infraction.

Note: The FIFA rule on charging the goalkeeper has been modified for youth, high school, and college soccer in the United States. At those levels of competition the goalkeeper may not be charged *at any time.*

Double Possession

The goalkeeper is considered to have legal possession when the ball is in her or his hands or cradled within the arms. An arm, leg, hand, or even finger placed on a stationary ball, bringing the ball under the goalkeeper's control, is considered legal possession. Opponents are not permitted to kick the ball once the goalkeeper has legal possession.

As of July 1991 the FIFA laws have also been amended to state that the goalkeeper will be considered in possession of the ball when he or she takes control of the ball by touching it with any part of his or her hands or arms. Possession now includes the goalkeeper's intentionally slapping the ball to her or his feet rather than catching it. The keeper does not have possession, however, when, in the opinion of the referee, the ball rebounds accidentally from the goalkeeper (for example, after the keeper has made a diving save).

This is a major rule change for goalkeepers. You can no longer purposely use your hands or arms to parry or slap the ball within range of your feet, dribble a few yards within the penalty area, and then pick up the ball. In the past goalkeepers commonly used this tactic to dribble the ball closer to the edge of the penalty area before distributing it, and also to waste time in games when their team was ahead in the score. Such action is now considered double possession, and the resulting penalty is the award of an indirect free kick to the opposing team at the point of the foul. It is important that it must be, in the opinion of the referee, a deliberate attempt by the goalkeeper to parry or slap the ball to the feet (rather than catch it), for the award of an indirect foul.

You must also understand that once you have possession of the ball and then release it, the ball must either leave the penalty area or be played by an opponent before you may again possess the ball with your hands.

Four-Step Rule

Once the goalkeeper has possession of the ball, he or she cannot take more than four steps without releasing it. Once the ball is released, the rules for double possession apply.

The four-step rule is designated to prevent the goalkeeper from intentionally wasting time or delaying the game. The referee has the authority to penalize a goalkeeper who uses actions or tactics for the purpose of delaying the game. The penalty for delay of game is an indirect free kick awarded the opposing team from the spot of the infraction.

Penalty Kick

When defending against a penalty kick, the goalkeeper must position with feet touching the goal line until the kicker's foot contacts the ball. The keeper may sway slightly back and forth but is not permitted to shout or distract the kicker by inordinate movements or motions—such action is considered poor conduct. (See the section on "Penalty Kicks" in chapter 10 for additional information.)

Glossary

attacker—The player with possession of the ball. Front running attackers are usually called strikers or wingers.

balance in defense—Positioning of defensive players that provides depth and support. Players nearest the ball mark opponents, while those away from the ball position to cover space.

baseball throw—A method of distribution used to toss the ball over medium distances.

blind-side run—A type of running off-the-ball in which a player without the ball runs outside of an opponent's field of vision in order to receive a pass.

block tackle—A defensive skill used to gain possession of the ball; the player uses the inside of the foot to block the ball away from an opponent.

boxing—A technique used to box, or punch, balls out of the goal area. Boxing skills are used when the goalkeeper is unsure of holding the ball.

breakaway—A situation where an attacker with the ball breaks free of defenders and creates a one-on-one situation with the goalkeeper.

concentration in defense—Positioning of defensive players to limit the space available to opponents in the most critical scoring areas.

counterattack—The initiation of an attack on the opposing goal upon gaining possession of the ball.

corner kick—A method of putting the ball into play after it has crossed the end line and was last touched by a member of the defending team.

cover—Defensive support. As a defender challenges for possession of the ball, she or he should be supported from behind (covered) by a teammate.

cross—A pass originating from the wing or flank area that is driven across the goalmouth.

defenders—A general term used to label the players positioned nearest to the goalkeeper. Most modern systems of play use three or four defenders.

diagonal run—A run designed to penetrate the defense while drawing defenders away from central positions.

direct kick—A free kick that can be scored without first touching another player.

distribution—Methods by which the goalkeeper initiates the attack after gaining control of the ball. The most common methods of distribution are throwing and kicking.

far post—The goalpost farthest from the ball.

flanks—Areas of the field near the touchlines that provide a narrow shooting angle to the goal.

forwards—Players who occupy the front attacking positions; usually identified as strikers and wingers.

four-step rule—Applies to the goalkeeper when in possession of the ball. The goalkeeper may not take more than four steps when in possession of the ball without releasing it to another player.

full volley—Striking the ball directly out of the air, most commonly with the instep of the foot.

functional training—Isolating for practice the techniques and tactics of specific player positions (such as the skill used by a goalkeeper to receive a high ball when under pressure of an opponent).

give-and-go pass—A combination pass where one player passes to a nearby teammate and then sprints forward to receive a return pass.

goal-side position—A defending player is positioned between his or her goal and the opponent to be marked.

grid—A confined area in which a small group of players practices skills and tactics.

half volley—Striking a dropping ball the instant it contacts the ground.

HEH principle—The goalkeeper's hands, eyes, and head should be in direct line with the ball as she or he receives it.

indirect kick—A free kick from which a goal cannot be scored directly. The ball must be touched by another player before entering the goal.

javelin throw—A method of goalkeeper distribution used to throw the ball over long distances.

marking—Tight coverage of an opponent.

near post—The goalpost nearest the ball.

one-touch passing—Interpassing among teammates without stopping the ball; also called first-time passing.

overlap—A method in which a supporting teammate runs from behind to a position ahead of the player with the ball; often used as a tactic to move defenders and midfielders into attacking positions.

penalty kick—A direct free kick awarded to the attacking team when a defending player commits a direct foul within her or his own penalty area. A penalty kick is taken from the penalty spot located 12 yards front and center of the goal. The goalkeeper must position with feet on the goal line until the ball is kicked.

poke tackle—A method in which a player reaches in and uses the toes to poke the ball away from an opponent.

ready position—The goalkeeper's basic stance when the ball is within shooting range of the goal.

restart—A method of initiating play after a stop in the action. Restarts include direct and indirect free kicks, throw-ins, corner kicks, goal kicks, and the drop ball.

running off-the-ball—Movement of a player without the ball that creates passing and scoring opportunities for teammates.

send off—To eject from play.

shielding—Positioning one's body between the opponent and the ball to maintain possession.

shoulder charge—A legal tactic used when challenging an opponent for the ball when the ball is within playing distance.

sidearm throw—A method of distribution used to toss the ball over short and medium distances.

slide tackle—A method in which a player slides and kicks the ball away from an opponent.

stopper back—A central defender, positioned in front of the sweeper back, who usually marks the opposing center striker.

striker—A front-running forward positioned in the central area of the field; usually one of the primary goal scorers on the team.

support—Movement of players into positions that provide passing options for the teammate with the ball.

sweeper back—The last field player in defense, who provides cover for the marking defenders.

system of play—Organization and responsibilities of the 10 field players.

tactics—Organizational concept, on individual, group, and team basis, of player roles within the team structure.

throw-in—A method of restarting play after the ball has traveled outside the touchlines. The ball must be held with two hands and released directly over the head. Both feet must be touching the ground when the ball is released.

touchline—A side boundary line.

two-touch passing—A type of interpassing in which the receiving player controls the ball with the first touch and passes to a teammate on the second.

wall pass—A combination pass with one player serving as a barrier to redirect the path of the ball. The player in possession passes off the ''wall'' and immediately sprints forward into open space to receive the return pass.

W catch—A position of the hands when catching the ball. Thumbs and forefingers are positioned behind the ball, while remaining fingers curl to the side of the ball.

width in attack—Using the width of the field in an attempt to draw defending players away from central positions. The objective is to create space in the most dangerous attacking zones.

wingbacks—Defenders positioned on the flanks who usually mark the opposing wing forwards.

winger—A front-running forward positioned in the flank area near the touchline.

zone defense—A system in which each player is responsible for defending a certain area of the field.

Index

Photos and illustrations are identified in italics.